# sinking of the MAYFLOWER

## lost november 12, 1912

# stephen weir

GSPH

Published by

GENERAL STORE
GSPH   PUBLISHING HOUSE INC.

1 Main Street, Burnstown, Ontario, Canada K0J 1G0
Telephone (613) 432-7697 or (613) 432-9385

ISBN 0-919431-42-9
Printed and bound in Canada

Cover design by Hugh Malcolm

Copyright © 1989
The General Store Publishing House Inc.
Burnstown, Ontario, Canada

## Canadian Cataloguing in Publication Data

Weir, Stephen
        The sinking of the Mayflower

Includes bibliographical references.
ISBN 0-919431-42-9

1. Mayflower (Paddlewheeler).  2. Temiskaming,
Lake, Region (Ont.) -- History.  3. Scuba diving--
Ontario -- Temiskaming, Lake -- Guide-books.
I. Title.

G530.M39W4 1989   971.3'44   C90-090072-5

First Printing January 1990

**To
Maria Nenadovich,
Michael and Andrew Weir.**

Thanks to *Diver Magazine*, Jean Ritchter, Arthur Rumleski, the Schuttes, Tim Legate, Howard Magda, Jack and Barbara Weir, Bruce Weir, Jasper Vanderhorst, Alvis Almeida, Bill Walker, Pam Bellefleur, Keith King, Bill McNeil, Geoff Ott and Brien Brotham.

# CHAPTER ONE

The body of a very special lady lies under the water, waiting. As each bleak year of her long, lonely vigil passes, piece after rotting piece of her broken corpse silently drifts away.

She died one bloody November evening, drowned at the hands of a howling wind. It was November 12, 1912, the night when death raced screaming into Renfrew County astride a frigid, north-east blow.

Out on the black waters of Kamaniskeg Lake the storm gripped the lady by her throat. Effortlessly, without mercy, the winter fury pushed the struggling woman into the near-frozen waters of the lake. Her last-breath bubbles were lost in a sea of froth whipped by the chilling winds of a frozen hell.

It was a quick fall to the sandy bottom of the lake. Here among the weeds and the schools of silent, grey fish, the body of the lady settled. Up above, the elements continued to rage, while below, at the grave site, it was peaceful — the woman had begun her wait.

There is a purpose in her stay. This decomposed corpse has held a lonely, watery death-watch, waiting for the strange mystery of her murder to be solved. The skeletal remains have a name, she is the *Mayflower*, queen of Lake Kamaniskeg, the homely matron of the Upper Ottawa Valley.

The *Mayflower* was a lady born of Ontario's pioneering days. A mistress of her times, the vessel's fate was tied to the march of progress, the civilizing of Eastern Ontario.

This is a true tale, a yarn that has the ingredients of a best-selling, thriller novel. The story charts a course littered with tragedy, human suffering and a body that absolutely refused to be buried.

The *Mayflower* was an ugly, wooden, stern-wheel paddle-ship that plied the waters of Lake Kamaniskeg. Made without thought to form or line, the seventy-seven-foot-long ship consisted of a rough, square, barn-like box sitting atop an almost flat hull. Built at the turn of this century, the ship travelled the waterways of this large lake which is part of the Madawaska River system, one hundred miles north-west of the city of Ottawa. The *Mayflower* made her mark by carrying passengers and freight and by shepherding long floating log booms.

**The steamship *Mayflower* from a photograph in the Public Archives.**

Built in 1903 in the village of Combermere, the principal town in the Township of Radcliffe, the ship was earmarked to carry corundum from a very large mine at nearby Craigmont to the rail-yard in Barry's Bay. Built by the Hudson brothers, who had owned and operated a number of freighters on the Madawaska River system, the 1903 ship, launched in 1904, replaced the *Hudson*, a steamer the men had built in 1900 and retired a scant four years later.

The Hudsons found it profitable servicing the corundum mines that lined the York River. Corundum, the hardest mineral next to diamond, was used in a number of

**The mining of corundum along the York River was a major industry at the turn of the century. Over two thousand people worked in the Craigmont mines in 1910.**
**Two ships, the *Tiger* and the *Ruby*, were kept busy hauling corundum barges from the mine to the rail-yards in Barry's Bay. The Hudson brothers were always eager to pick up cargo from mines such as the above-pictured Bangor Corundum Mine, Craigmont. The picture was taken in the 1900-1910 time-frame.**

Photograph — the Ontario Archives 2771 55056

manufacturing processes including the making of glass and fine pottery. In their day, the mineral deposits along the York and Madawaska Rivers were considered the largest known deposits, not only in Canada, but the world.

The ships that the Hudson brothers owned were kept busy ferrying the crystals from the mine to the railway yard... at least until 1904. That was the year the Hudsons launched the *Mayflower*. About a month after the *Mayflower* splashed into the waters of the Kamaniskeg, so too did two new competing steamers. The owners of the mine started using their own mini-steamships, the *Ruby* and the *Tiger*, forcing the *Mayflower's* owners to find other business. The Hudsons took to carrying passengers, mail and freight to keep the steamship operation a going concern.

If the *Mayflower* had stayed an ore carrier she would have lived and died in total obscurity. It was the switch to the passenger-carrying mode that gave the *Mayflower* her notoriety — her mysterious demise won her a place high on the list of Renfrew County disasters.

Never heard of the *Mayflower*? Then you probably have never had the opportunity to hoist a brew or two at the Balmoral Hotel near Lake Kamaniskeg. It never fails, when you have a draft in the taproom of that Barry's Bay hotel the talk will eventually swing to the tale of the *Mayflower* and how four men clung to life on the top of a dead man's coffin.

Now, some taverns have paintings of nude women hanging over their bars. Not so in Barry's Bay. This rural Ontario hostelry has an oil painting that shows, in graphic detail, four people clinging to a floating coffin.

The lost souls are adrift in the frothing waters of Lake Kamaniskeg. It is November 12, 1912, and the wooden stern-wheeler, the *Mayflower*, has already sunk beneath the near-freezing surface of this large Ontario lake.

Three of the four men in the painting were the only survivors.[1] The ship went down so fast that only one of the four had a chance to put on a life-jacket. They had to

[1] *One of the four, Paddy O'Brien, died from exposure while waiting to be rescued. A fifth man, Aaron Parcher, survived the sinking of the* **Mayflower.** *The pilot of the ill-fated ship, he donned an inner-tube life-jacket and swam towards shore to get help. He died shortly before or after reaching shore. Relatives of the dead man say that he died from a ruptured stomach.*

grab for whatever flotsam they could find — when a coffin drifted by, the quartet grabbed a hold and set out for land, as depicted in the hotel painting.

The patrons of the Balmoral have had years of Friday nights to learn the history of the sinking of the *Mayflower*. Locals can tell you how nine people drowned when the stern-wheeler suddenly sank to the bottom of the lake, just a few miles from the hotel. However, while the bare facts are known by many, most people haven't had time to take an in-depth look into the loss of that ship.

Scuba divers have. Donning underwater gear and plunging into the waters of Kamaniskeg is the only way to look at the *Mayflower* now. Twenty feet below the surface, on the sand bottom of this clean lake, rests the shattered remains of the *Mayflower*.

Up above, the surface of the lake is usually calm. The water over the wreck is not deep and the shore is, for a good swimmer, not far away. It is hard to believe that nine people drowned when she suddenly sank down to this, her watery grave. It is an easy wreck to find and to dive, and that has made the *Mayflower* a favourite attraction for the underwater set.

Now as sunken hulks go, there isn't all that much to view. It is the story behind the moss-covered remains that makes the wreck worth visiting.

Back in the 1900s the Hudson family was the life-blood of the Combermere community: John Hudson was the township's first and only reeve, he and his brother Hal owned a lumber-yard, his mother ran one of the village's better hotels and the *Mayflower* was the village's link to Barry's Bay to the north-east and to Palmer Rapids, Craigmont and Havergal to the south-west . Havergal was a docking point for steamships on the York River.

Beyond this point the shallow waters of the muddy York began to run rough through a series of impassable rapids.[2]

As a free-lance steamer, the Hudson ship was vital to the community. When the *Mayflower* wasn't hauling freight, the Hudsons offered her services for pleasure trips and moonlight cruises. Many a toddy was consumed in her hold as men gathered for what was literally a floating card game.

According to the *Ottawa Citizen*, Hudson had been able to put seventy people on board the seventy-seven-foot craft if he stretched his resources to the limit. The dozen on board November 12, 1912, was the norm.

Despite her many uses, the *Mayflower* managed to follow a schedule of sorts. She usually made one round trip a day from Combermere to Barry's Bay and back. On occasion she would make two runs a day but, since she carried no adequate lights, the double voyage had to be made in daylight. By fall, when the sun set early in the day, the *Mayflower* could only make one and a half trips a day. The ship often started the day in Combermere and ended it in Barry's Bay and the next day would start in Barry's Bay and end in either Combermere or Palmer Rapids.

On November 12, 1912, the *Mayflower* strayed from her usual pattern. She travelled the route twice, making her second trip back to Barry's Bay to pick up a special cargo. She didn't leave port for the last leg of the second run until hours after she was usually at home in her berth in Combermere.

[2] *Today, all that can be seen of the steamship activity at Havergal is a huge iron ring fused into the rocks on the York River bank. The **Ruby, Tiger** and **Mayflower** would tie up to that ring.*

The reason for the delay? A tardy coffin. John Brown was a local resident who had recently died in Yorkton, Saskatchewan. Thirty-five-year-old Robert Pachal, the dead man's brother-in-law, was bringing the body back to be buried in a hamlet near Combermere. The train, delivering the body and its guardian, arrived late in Barry's Bay and *Mayflower* owner John Hudson returned from Combermere late in the day to fetch the cargo.

When the *Mayflower* left Barry's Bay around the supper hour there were thirteen people on board — twelve of them alive. Two hours later, in the midst of a strong winter blow, the ship went down. Nine people, including owner John Hudson, died; three men and the coffin were saved.

The loss of the *Mayflower* put the reputation of Jack Hudson and the industrial fate of the community on trial. What follows is the history of that ship, her demise, and the subsequent inquest that solved the mystery of the *Mayflower*.

# CHAPTER TWO

Would you sail with a man who was a rumoured drunk, who had a boat sink under him and had a village burn around him? If a soul can be tainted, John Hudson, the owner of the *Mayflower*, had broken mirrors, black cats and the number thirteen tattooed on his psyche.

The *Mayflower* became an underwater attraction through a series of weird occurrences. It was a matter of bad luck piling up so quickly that it buried John Hudson. The weight of his ill fortune took the hapless, Renfrew County pioneer to the bottom with his ugly ship.

**A view of Barry's Bay at the turn of the century.**

Post Card Photograph — Arthur Rumleski Collection

If the fates aren't to be blamed for the sinking of that ship and the subsequent loss of nine lives, then there is a whole menu of sins that it can all be blamed upon. Include in that litany of misfortune the following: unforgiving weather, a poorly maintained ship, improper modifications to the stern-wheel's paddles, weak government control on shipping inspections, a wayward life-raft and a tardy coffin.

If the passengers of the *Mayflower* had known how ill-fated Jack (as the locals used to call John Hudson) had been in the past year and a half, they were probably betting that he was due for a run of good luck. They guessed wrong. Hudson's fortunes came in threes; the events of November 12, 1912, were the third roll of Hudson's dice.

Water and fire chased J. C. Hudson. A year and a half earlier, the family hotel built by his late father, John Hudson Sr., burned to the ground.

The Hudson Inn had been run by Jack's mother, Elizabeth, since her husband's death in 1900. It was a large wooden building constructed in the 1860s. The Hudson family had been rebuilding the village landmark in 1911 at the time of the fire. They had dreams of building a summer retreat and fishing lodge, with the *Mayflower* carrying vacationers to and from her door.

When smoke was spotted billowing out of the inn, the hamlet's volunteer brigade could do little to save the roadside hostelry. They were soon too busy soaking down the roofs of their own homes to worry about the local hotel.

The Hudson Inn was the first Combermere building to fall under the sparks and smoke, but it wasn't the last. Before the final wall had fallen, the sky over the village was crimson, lit by the flaming walls of other houses and businesses in the neighbourhood. According to the newspaper reports of the day, the fire 'swept away half the village.'

Jack Hudson didn't let a mishap like that singe his dream. He and his brother Henry built the brick New British Hotel on top of the charred ruins of that first establishment.

Perhaps their recovery was made easier by the family's previous experience with disaster. Three months before the fire, Jack and his brother Henry (Hal) had the very damp experience of having the *Mayflower* sink from under their feet.

It was a warm, Ottawa Valley day. Jack and Hal's home-built steamer chugged along the Madawaska River heading towards Combermere under clear blue skies. She was nearing the home hamlet when a submerged deadhead pierced her hull.

Floating logs were always of concern to the half-dozen or so large craft that travelled the waters of Lake Kamaniskeg and the Madawaska River. The river had long been used by the lumber barons to transport logs from the Upper Ottawa Valley down to their yards in Arnprior, Ottawa and Hull. The last big log drive on the Madawaska was in September 1911, just months after the *Mayflower* had her losing encounter with a log.

"It was a tree that had fallen in years previous," Henry Edward Hudson was later to explain. "The boat had to make this turn and run close to the shore of the stream. This tree was sixty or eighty feet long and according, as the boat went over it, it had worked up, and this morning, when we were going up (sic), the west wind caught her and the tree made a hole in her and she sank. She went down."

**The *Mayflower* first sank in 1911 while travelling down the narrow Madawaska River near Combermere. The river was still being used to transport logs to mills in Arnprior and Ottawa — deadheads and maverick logs were a constant danger to shipping. This photograph was taken near where the *Mayflower* went down after striking a submerged tree trunk.**

Photograph — S. Weir

It took a scant four minutes for the pine and oak vessel to settle on the river bottom. That was time enough for the captain to steer his sinking freighter close to shore. The pride of Lake Kamaniskeg became the wreck of the Madawaska, but not before the fifteen people on board had scrambled into the life-raft and watched from afar as she disappeared under the surface of the tea-coloured river.

John and Henry had planned for just such an emergency. The *Mayflower* had a large lifeboat — Renfrew County style. It was thirty feet in length and, with a depth of only twenty inches, was near to the water. The life-raft was a flat, lumberman's pointer, originally designed to be used on shallow, fast-moving rivers. Loggers needed a platform that was untippable (by virtue of its size) and could float in knee-deep streams. The *Mayflower's* pointer-cum-life-raft could carry close to twenty passengers safely.

The pointer was a functional piece of equipment for the *Mayflower*. The paddle-wheel steamer travelled a route that took her to very shallow waterways — both the Madawaska and York Rivers had stretches where a man could stand on the bottom and still wear a dry shirt. When the *Mayflower* came into one of these areas and had to land a passenger or freight , the big pointer was untied from the stern and manhandled toward land.

**Part of the *Mayflower's* route took her down the York River to the corundum mines near Craigmont. The Madawaska River is, for the most part, a fast-moving, narrow, easy-to-navigate waterway. The York River (which drains out of the Madawaska and flows towards Bancroft), on the other hand, is a wide, shallow, swampy river. Passage from Combermere to the mine was, in the heat of the summer, difficult. Pictured is Conroy's Marsh near the junction of the Madawaska and York Rivers.**

Photograph — S. Weir

Back in 1911, M.R. Davis was the inspector of hulls and equipment for the Federal Department of Marine and Fisheries. He described the lifeboat of the *Mayflower* thusly: "They had four oars belonging to the boat, and a bailing dish and an axe goes with the boat."

Most passenger ships lashed their life-rafts onto the roof or deck of their ships: the *Mayflower* crew used their pointer too often to allow the luxury of stowing it away. Under Canadian shipping laws, a vessel the size of the *Mayflower* needed only one life-raft . That raft, regardless of size, should have, in most waterways, been kept on board — the *Mayflower* dragged its pointer from a stern line.

When the *Mayflower* went down that first time in 1911 the crew and the paying customers climbed into the overgrown wooden raft and watched with wide-eyed amusement as shipwreck history was made in the Upper Ottawa Valley.

The records are sketchy as to the exact date of her first sinking. It appears that she went down in late May or early June of 1911. She didn't stay on the bottom of the river for very long.

A year after the first sinking, Ottawa's *The Evening Journal* wrote about the mishap. "It was thought that the *Mayflower* would be left on the bottom, Captain Jack Hudson thought otherwise. He got together a gang of men, constructed outfits on either side of the sunken craft, passed chains under her and with a set of jack screws, brought the boat to the top again."

When the ship was back on the surface, Jack Hudson prepared to return her to active service. His brother, maybe sensing the frailty of the *Mayflower*, sold his share of the ship to Jack. And the ship's master, Captain McGlade, handed in his resignation at the end of the 1911 season.

Jack Hudson was able to bring a wreck back to the surface and he was able to rebuild a burned-out hotel. His ability to outrun everlasting disaster ran short on November 12, 1912.

**The east-bound Grand Trunk train was photographed near Algonquin Park in 1910. It could well have been the train that carried Brown's body to Golden Lake where it would have been transfered onto the Golden Lake-to-Barry's Bay line.**

Photograph — Ontario Archives S13829

# CHAPTER THREE

A dead man doesn't have a qualm about waiting for a ride on a freighter, a corpse has all the time in the world. On the other hand, a steamship that tarries for a coffin courts disaster. *Mayflower* owner Jack Hudson made an unscheduled return to Barry's Bay to pick up a coffin and wound up losing his life for his troubles.

The *Mayflower* was a flat-bottomed craft that was meant to be run only during daylight hours. There were no permanent running

**John Brown, the man inside the coffin.**

Photograph — the Schutt Collection

lights to help the crew steer past the treacherous passageways of Lake Kamaniskeg and the Madawaska River. None of the waist-deep, shallow shoals were properly marked for night travel. During daytime voyages, the ship's pilot was on the alert looking for errant logs that broke from the floating booms — an impossible task to tackle after sundown.

Hudson didn't mind living on the wrong side of the safety rules. He operated his seventy-seven-foot *Mayflower* all summer and fall in 1912 without proper government papers and without a certified captain at the helm.

He once made it a rule that he would never run the *Mayflower* at night, save for his popular midnight cruises that took place within sight and safety of the home

**Although recently restored to its original state, the Barry's Bay station no longer sees passenger trains arrive and depart. The station is across the tracks from the Balmoral Hotel.**

Photograph — S. Weir

harbour. He broke that personal commandment when John Brown's coffin arrived late in Barry's Bay aboard the Grand Trunk Railroad (GTR).

The GTR operated a spur line from Golden Lake through the village of Wilno and on into Barry's Bay. Passengers and freight coming from the west or up from Ottawa caught a morning ride from Golden Lake to Barry's Bay. The train left Ottawa at 7:45 a.m. and arrived near the Barry's Bay Balmoral Hotel at 12:50 p.m., giving passengers plenty of time to catch the afternoon boat ride to Combermere.

On Tuesday, November 12, the 7:45 was delayed, so much so that Hudson decided to go ahead with his trip

**Situated right beside the now defunct Barry's Bay train station, the Balmoral was the perfect way point for travellers to wait for the *Mayflower*. They could dine in the hotel and wait for the departure of the *Mayflower*. The town dock was a five-minute buggy drive from the hotel.**

Photograph — S. Weir

before the train arrived. He left word at the station that any
Combermere-bound passengers (and the coffin) would
probably have to wait until Wednesday to make the
voyage because a storm was approaching.

**Tailor William Boehme's Combermere gravestone.**

Photograph — S. Weir

When the train finally arrived, Robert Pachal, the coffin custodian, phoned William Boehme in Combermere and asked him to convince Hudson to return the *Mayflower* to Barry's Bay to ferry the body back to the grieving family.

Boehme, a local tailor, was more than just a neighbour and friend to Jack Hudson. Both men were members of the Radcliffe Township Council, Hudson the reeve, Boehme a councillor. Boehme, a relative of Brown's, quickly convinced Hudson to return to Barry's Bay. He in turn asked two Combermere friends, Paddy O'Brien and William Murphy to join them on their solemn journey. The three and another paying customer, salesman Harry Leach, boarded the boat and set off with Hudson and his crew of two on their sombre mission.

Jack Hudson had taken his first giant step towards doom the day before the ship actually sank. On Monday, November 11, 1912, Hudson was on the bridge when his *Mayflower* chugged up to the Barry's Bay dock. It was late in the day and according to his brother, Henry Hudson, there were twelve tons of cargo in the ship's hold.

The crew was able to dock the stern-wheeler but not without incident. The large, crude pointer, which was dragged from the stern of the *Mayflower*, broke free and drifted out towards the lake.

Hudson, worn out from his journey and faced with the prospect of unloading his ship in the cold weather, did not reattach his life-raft to the rear of his ship. Instead it was retrieved and lashed to the town wharf.

The weather was beginning to turn ugly. It had already snowed that month, everyone could feel it in their bones that winter was approaching. The nights were long and noticeably colder. For travellers wishing to reach Combermere and the rich mining communities to the south, the choices were limited. There was an axle-breaking trail that ran from the Bay to Combermere where it linked up with the Peterson Settlement Road from the Maynooth district and the Opeongo Road from down Renfrew way.[3]

The pioneer road was best taken in the winter when a blanket of ice and snow covered the ruts, bumps and hollows. In the spring, summer and fall the route took a day to complete. Its mudholes, tree falls and insects made the prospect of a three-hour ride on the *Mayflower* seem like a luxurious treat.

A trip on the *Mayflower* cost $1.50 one way. Children, when Jack Hudson decided to charge, paid fifty cents. Sounds cheap? It wasn't. On May 17, 1912, a Pembroke Hotel

**The Combermere Post Office was, at the turn of the century, located on the banks of the Madawaska River.**

Photograph — Arthur Rumleski Collection

[3] *Even during the 1920s, the road link between the two towns was very bad. In 1929 it would take, on average, two hours to drive from Barry's Bay to Combermere, a distance of fifteen miles!*

announced that its prices were going up. A week's board at the inn was set at $5.00 and if a guest wanted full-course dinners, a forty-cent-per-meal charge was added to the bill.

Travellers arriving on the GTR at the track-side village of Barry's Bay could lunch in Simon Finesty's Balmoral Hotel. It was Jack Hudson's habit to call in at the public house before departing from the village wharf. Phone service was in place and travellers could book ahead at Hudson's hotel in Combermere.

On the morning of the twelfth, Hudson left the Balmoral early and went to supervise the unloading of his ship. By 9:00 a.m. the fireman, J. Tom Delaney, had stoked the boiler full with a load of light, pine slabs — the *Mayflower* was ready to make the home trip to Combermere.

**The *Mayflower* would sound her whistle as she approached the swinging Combermere Bridge. That would give his family time to run out of the hotel and move the bridge so the captain wouldn't have to stop the unwieldy, stern-wheel ship.**

Photograph — Arthur Rumleski Collection

The ship's schedule was not so precise that the locals would dare set their watches to it. Still, her pattern in life would have caused her to do one of two things that Tuesday.

She would normally have made a late-morning or early-afternoon trip to Combermere and Palmer Rapids and if the demand was there, she would have headed up the shallow, leech-infested York River to Havergal and then back to Combermere, where she would berth until the next day. If there was sufficient daylight and paying freight, the *Mayflower* might have steamed back to Barry's Bay, where she would remain until the following morning.

**An aerial picture of the Combermere/Madawaska River bridge facing north towards Lake Kamaniskeg. Barry's Bay is at the top right of the picture. The Hudson Hotel is at the right of the bridge, hidden by a number of large trees. This photograph was taken November 10, 1967. The hamlet has grown considerably since then.**

Photograph — The Ontario Archives NE 4-2-1067

On November 12, on what was to be Jack Hudson's last day on the face of the earth, the *Mayflower* made her morning trip from Barry's Bay to Combermere without incident. Hudson was all set to berth his ship for the night but was convinced by his neighbour and fellow councillor, William Boehme, to return to Barry's Bay. Boehme agreed to travel to Barry's Bay with the vessel. Hudson was probably happy to learn that the two would not travel alone — Paddy O'Brien, William Murphy and at least one paying customer, a salesman, were also booked for the on-again, off-again return leg.

Harry Leach was the Ottawa-bound salesman who decided to catch the Barry's Bay boat ride. He wanted to get to the train station as quickly as possible. Leach had been on the *Mayflower* before and had a very low opinion of the ship's worthiness and Hudson's ability to captain her. Despite his concerns, Leach boarded the ship feeling that it was the only way he was going to be able to make his capital-city connection.

He was later to say, at the *Mayflower* inquest, that the look of the ship frightened him. "I didn't have any faith in the boat," he testified, "in common with a great many others, as it was not a boat that inspired confidence."

"It would be somewhere about two-thirty, probable (*sic*) near three o'clock when the *Mayflower* left Combermere for Barry's Bay to pick up the coffin and the nine paying passengers." continued the James Street, Ottawa resident.

His trust in the *Mayflower* had been shaken, not only by the crude look of the rough-timbered vessel, but also by the way Hudson handled her. The Barry's Bay landing, where Leach got off for good, was not an award-winning performance.

While Hudson was docking the box-shaped *Mayflower,* she crashed into the *Ruby*[4] at the Barry's Bay dock. The *Ruby's* crew were able to push off the *Mayflower*, so the collision did little or no damage to either ship.

Leach left the waterfront at six o'clock and made his way to the Balmoral Hotel where he booked himself a room for the night. He then shared a meal with four salesmen who would soon be boarding the *Mayflower* to make that special night run back to Combermere. Leach complained about the ride he had taken and the bumpy docking, however his comments failed to convince the men to cancel their lake voyage. His dinner companions begged his leave and went to board the *Mayflower*.

Meanwhile, back at the dock, Hudson was quickly readying his vessel for the night journey. The coffin carrying John H. Brown was hauled aboard by his brother-in-law, Robert Pachal, his uncle, William Boehme, Mr. Murphy and by Hudson. It was left, untied, on the outside deck.

Once the coffin was aboard, Hudson had the *Mayflower's* syphon pump turned on. Had the mild collision with the steamer *Ruby* caused a leak?

[4] *The **Ruby** and her sister ship, the **Tiger**, were owned and operated by the Ontario Corundum Company Limited. They were used to push corundum barges from the mines near the York River to the rail-yard in Barry's Bay. The **Ruby** was forty-one feet long, nine feet wide, and had a draft of four feet. She had a single-screw engine and was built by the same man who helped Hudson build his **Mayflower**. The last owner of the **Ruby** was Henry Hudson, who retired her in 1919. The **Tiger**, built in 1896, was a smaller vessel. She was thirty-four feet long and seven-and-a-half feet wide with a three-foot draft. The **Tiger** was a single-screw vessel built in Lakeport, USA.*

The captain and the two-member crew waited for their passengers to finish their meals and join the ship. The three had ample time to untie the life-raft which was lashed to the dock and reattach it to the stern of the *Mayflower*. They didn't, and when the passengers finally boarded ship and Hudson sailed, the life-raft remained at port in Barry's Bay.

The big lifeboat wasn't left behind out of simple neglect. The pointer was used to ferry passengers from the *Mayflower* to shore whenever the stern-wheeler couldn't dock. Since the nine passengers and the pine box were headed for Combermere and Palmer Rapids, the heavy, wooden life-raft wouldn't be needed. The thing was a massive affair, twenty people could easily sit in her — by leaving it behind Hudson was sloughing off dead weight; the *Mayflower* would make better time *sans* pointer.

The shape of the *Mayflower* was by no means aerodynamic. In a strong head wind the *Mayflower*, even with a full steam in her Fitzgibbon boiler, could be bodily pushed backwards. The wind was up that night and the pointer was an anchor better left behind. Besides, there were thirty life-jackets on board that blustery night.

It was dark at seven o'clock when the steamer finally pushed away from the Barry's Bay wharf. The stars shone brightly, the air was bitterly cold and a strong wind was blowing out of the north. The paying customers stayed indoors — who would want to brave the freezing winds just to share deck space with a coffin? The body of Brown, the thirteenth on board the ship, was the finishing touch to what was shaping up to be a horror-filled evening.

The mere listing of the names of the dead and those that were hurt in the calamity does little to explain why the terrible accident deeply hurt the soul of the Renfrew County community. To understand the loss, one must examine the make-up of the twelve living souls and one body that sailed out onto the dark waters of Lake Kamaniskeg that night.

Captain Jack Hudson was a tall, strong man. With dark hair and a handle-bar moustache, the *Mayflower* owner cut an imposing figure.

Hudson was the sort of man who walked about town with a smile permanently on his face. He was known throughout the Renfrew Valley thanks to his shipping business, the hotel and due in no small part to his political endeavours. As the reeve of Radcliffe Township, he also sat on the county council in Pembroke where he was a

**Above left, a charcoal drawing of Aaron Parcher, the crew member who tried to swim for help after the *Mayflower* sank. Above right, Mrs. Maude Parcher. This picture of Aaron Parcher's widow was taken at the age of eighty-six, decades after the sinking.**

Photographs — Jean Richter Collection

voice for the people of the Kamaniskeg district. One of the last things he did in Pembroke was to push loudly for the county to help Radcliffe Township build a new bridge. In 1912, at county council, Hudson was named the head of the Court of Revision.

He and his thirty-five-year-old wife, Margaret Mahon, had an eight-year-old son named Edward. When they married on May 4, 1903, it was the social event of the year. Hudson, the Anglican county councillor, wed the daughter of Barry's Bay's John Mahon in the Bishop's Palace in Pembroke. Bishop Lorrain conducted the Roman Catholic ceremony.

Twenty-six-year-old Aaron Parcher was the *Mayflower's* pilot and Hudson's first mate. Aaron was a handsome young man. He had brown hair and sported a short, well-groomed moustache.

Parcher was married and he and his wife Maude had two children, four-year-old Gordon and two-year-old Allen. Aaron Parcher and his young family lived with his father Cyrus, on a farm alongside the Madawaska River, just a mile or two from Combermere.

Ironically, Parcher was planning for the voyage to be one of his last trips on the *Mayflower*. He and his wife had purchased a farm in the Kirkland Lake district and planned to move the family there at the end of the shipping season. He had polished his hunting rifle[5] and left it at his father's farm. Parcher planned to go hunting the day after the *Mayflower* was tied up for the winter. After the hunt it was 'goodbye Combermere and hello Kirkland Lake.'

Little is known of the fireman, Tom Delaney, save for the fact that the poor chap couldn't swim. Historians feel that the

[5] *The rifle has been kept by Parcher's family.*

young man was an orphan with no relatives in the Renfrew County area. There is no mention in the reports of the day that he was married. He had the hardest job on the ship. The *Mayflower's* boiler had a hunger for wood, and Delaney had to feed the fire every eight to ten minutes.

There were nine passengers, four travellers, four locals and Pachal aboard. The four travellers were Ottawa based salesmen. Back in 1912 sales representatives were known as 'travellers.'

The travellers were: a salesman for F.L. Castle Company, twenty-seven-year-old George Bothwell; a fifty-six-year-old salesman for Curticle Silk of Ottawa, Gordon Peverly; a Canadian Consolidated Rubber Company representative, James Harper and J.S. "John" Imlach, a traveller for the General Supply Company.

The local passengers included William Boehme, Mrs. William McWhirter, Patrick O'Brien and William Murphy.

Boehme and O'Brien were both solid pillars in the Combermere community. Boehme, a fifty-eight-year-old tailor, was one of the original settlers in the area. Back in 1860, when the Crown published its first map of the area, Boehme is shown as having property just a stone's throw from the Hudson family.

Many of the original landowners in the district had their land grants witnessed by the well-liked tailor.

Patrick, or Paddy, O'Brien was a big, stout man, a figure befitting the role of innkeeper. "Paddy O'Brien owned a hotel in Purdy first where loggers and lumbermen would stay," wrote Purdy journalist Jean Richter. "At that time a road through the wilderness to the settlement called Centreview was well travelled and is yet called the Paddy Road... Paddy then bought the hotel in Combermere from my step-grandmother Roxanne Parcher Watt. There was a bar in Paddy O'Brien's hotel and a spittoon at every stool. One could buy a glass of booze or a bottle and a glass and drink it right there."

Paddy O'Brien was married to Tilly Price. The couple had at least four children: Howie, Walter, Babe and Matie. Aside from the hotel, the family ran the town's phone system.

Mrs. William McWhirter was an eighty-year-old grandmother from Fort Stewart. She left two sons, William and Thomas, both of RR 2 Bancroft. The grandmother had been visiting relatives in Bristol, Quebec. She had intended to take a coach home, but when she learned that the *Mayflower* was going to sail she bought herself a ticket.

William Murphy was a resident of the hamlet of Rockingham, where he lived with his sister. The two are now buried side by side in an untended Rockingham graveyard.

The deaths of the people who sailed on the *Mayflower* have been well documented by the three travellers who survived to see the morning of November the 13th.

Five people survived the sinking, but only three lived to tell their tale. All three were from Ottawa. They were Gordon Peverly, James Harper and J. S. "John" Imlach. Their stories were told to the press only hours after their rescue from the frozen bank of Gull Island. One month after the tragedy, two of the lucky trio made much longer statements at a federal government inquest held to investigate the sinking of the *Mayflower*.

"We left for Combermere in the neighbourhood of seven o'clock, it might be (*sic*) shortly after seven and we stayed inside the boat around in different positions." recalled Ottawa traveller Gordon Peverly.

"It was not a stormy night when we left Barry's Bay. A little way down the river (Lake Kamaniskeg) however, it began to blow," remembered Peverly. "(It was blowing) when we got through to the Narrows, about six miles from Barry's Bay."

Keeping indoors, Peverly, Harper and fellow salesman George Bothwell spent most of the voyage huddled around the boiler, swapping the tales that travellers told. They were joined every eight minutes by the engineer-cum-fireman, young Tom Delaney. The lad had to split his time between monitoring the 13.5 HP engine and stuffing slabs of pine into the boiler's fire-box. The pine was freshly cut. The sparks and constant crackles kept the passengers' attention away from the howling winds outside.

The breeze was at the *Mayflower's* back and the ship made good time as she travelled up Barry's Bay towards the main body of the lake. The lights of the town lit her stern while her bow plunged into the dim, starlit darkness.

Her passageway through the islands that clutter the entrance to the Narrows was quick. Two hours after she left the wharf the stern-wheeler entered the safe, deep waters where the Madawaska River and Lake Kamaniskeg merge.

"It went on towards nine o'clock and I asked the Engineer ... Delaney, I think his name was, what time we would get to Combermere and he asked me what time it was," said Gordon Peverly. "I took out my watch and said it was around nine o'clock, and he said we would get up there about ten o'clock, and it wasn't five minutes after that till we saw water rushing in both sides of the stairs and we scrambled to the front of the boat and were taken down with her."

Joseph Harper, the Canadian Consolidated Rubber Company shoe salesman, remembered the sinking vividly. "I was standing right at the door near the boilers when it happened."

The *Mayflower* had two doorways, port and starboard. The openings were without proper doors, which accounts for the men having to huddle around the boiler. "There was a board or something across the bottom of the doorways but the top of them were open," recalled Harper.

"The first thing I noticed was the water coming in the door right where we were standing... it came in very rapidly, we didn't wait to see, I didn't wait to see, I ran right forward."

Harper, a newly-wed, had good reason to be frightened. He couldn't swim a stroke and had not planned to be on the water in a steamship in the first place.

Harper had moved to Ottawa from Kinburn in 1910. He had been working for the rubber company for two years and had a weekly route through the Barry's Bay/Combermere territory. He knew the condition of the *Mayflower* and had probably sailed on her before.

On the night the *Mayflower* sank, Nellie, his wife, who was waiting for him back in Ottawa, received a letter from him saying that he planned to drive from Barry's Bay to Combermere. His change of mind almost cost him his life.

John S. Imlach was a young salesman working for the General Supply Company. A bachelor at the age of twenty-nine, he lived with his parents who, as operators of the Ottawa-based Victoria Foundry Company, were members of the industrial establishment in the capital city.

"We were sitting in the engine room talking with Mr. Bothwell, when suddenly we noticed water coming in. Within fifteen seconds the boat filled with water up to the cabin," said Imlach in an interview with a *Canadian Press* reporter.

Peverly, on the other hand, told his story to the *Toronto Star* and in an exclusive interview went to great lengths to describe that moment of hell. "I *(sic)* with George Bothwell and Joe Harper was standing in the engine room.

We rushed up forward to try to get an old lady, but the water came in and the boat settled at the stern and broke her back. I remember, though, diving through a window after calling to Harper and Bothwell. Harper answered but Bothwell didn't."

The brown, cold waters of Lake Kamaniskeg came pouring into the cabin through the side doors and from the stern-wheel's open box. She was a flat-bottomed boat with a heavy stern and was designed to sail with a heavy load in the bow area. Since she was travelling light that night, there was nothing to counterbalance the weight of the engine, wheel and boiler — when her integrity was breached there was nothing that could keep her afloat save for the air inside her.

Peverly managed to get back onto the deck of the ship which at that point was still above water — though barely. It was then that the salesman ran into Hudson, or vice versa as his testimony indicates:

"We all made a run to the front of the boat. I slipped or tripped some way and fell and when I got on my feet again, Captain Hudson he ran back and knocked me off my feet the second time. I was the last man off that part of the boat and as I got up I saw him (Hudson) back at the pipes at the engine by the wheel."

Captain Hudson was apparently trying to open the steam valves to save the *Mayflower's* boiler. That was the last time he was seen alive. A diver sent onto the wreck two days later found Hudson's body near those same steam valves; he died trying to save his beloved *Mayflower*.

Harper and Imlach were ahead of Peverly. "Mr. Harper went right through the boat and Mr. Imlach got a hold of the old lady (Mrs. McWhirter) and he was endeavouring to put a lifebelt on her, and I had the feeling that the boat was going down," continued Peverly.

"I told him (Imlach) to grab a lantern and I (Peverly) would take the old lady. We went on and there came another lurch and the boat went right down."

Over the years, a legend has developed about the fate of eighty-year-old Mrs. William McWhirter. The story tells how she gave up her life-jacket to Mr. Harper saying that a younger person deserved a chance to live. Harper did end up with a life-jacket. At the inquest it was reported there were over thirty life jackets on board — enough for all the passengers three times over. In Ottawa's *The Evening Journal*, Imlach is quoted as saying, " We did everything we could to save the old lady who was on the boat... we had to let go the old lady on account of her terrible struggling and the grip she took of us."

The body of Mrs. McWhirter was recovered by a government-hired diver inside the *Mayflower*. She wasn't wearing a life-jacket.

When the *Mayflower* gave that last gasp and settled onto the bottom, three people drowned immediately: Mrs. McWhirter, Bothwell and Hudson. Imlach, Harper, Peverly and O'Brien stood on top of the wheel-house waist deep in cold water. Aaron Parcher, the pilot, stood with them briefly.

Parcher hadn't been hired as the pilot on the basis of any formal training. Instead the twenty-six-year-old worked for Hudson because he knew the waters around Combermere. It was his home turf, so to speak. When the *Mayflower* sank, she went down within sight of Parcher's father's house.

The power of the cold wind continued to mount. Luckily for the men stranded on the wheel-house and for those in the water, there was little chop along the surface of the lake. Parcher, wearing a life-jacket, could easily make out his family home four or five hundred feet away.

"I live right opposite here and I can make shore and bring out a boat," yelled Aaron Parcher to the passengers in the water. With that he set out to swim home.

Parcher was a hero. He swam so hard against the wind blowing offshore that he died. According to his family, Parcher died of a stomach rupture.

His fourteen-year-old brother Howard was out walking the next morning when he spotted Aaron's hat floating in the water. A minute later he found his brother's corpse floating only a step from dry land.

Howard got his brother Simon and his father Cyrus, and the body was pulled from the water. They now knew that something terrible had happened on board the *Mayflower*.

Word was sent to Hudson's family and the search began.

When Parcher set out for land, the four salesmen were standing on top of the wreck. There were two men clinging to the flag-pole a few feet from them. They were Murphy and Delaney. Boehme and Pachal floundered in the water as they tried to paddle their way to the relative safety of the men on the pilot-house. The weight of their soaking clothes, the cold water and the strong winds worked mightily against them.

"I had a lifebelt, but I didn't have time to get it on properly and I climbed up on the rail of the boat and I think the air from the cabin held her there for a few seconds and during that time I took the opportunity of putting the lifebelt on properly," recounted Joseph Harper at the inquest. "She lurched and I caught the rough box over to Mr. Peverly and Mr. Imlach and Mr. O'Brien were all there ... we stood there for a little while and we decided we couldn't stay there all night and we drifted on the coffin for a while."

"We made an attempt to get Delaney who was on the flag-staff," said Peverly, picking up the tale. "There was a flag-staff at the front of the boat and we tried to get him there, and there were two others we saw drown between us and them.

"Murphy was one of the two who drowned I am almost certain... the other man I think was Boehme. But I couldn't say for sure," continued Peverly.

"We got to within about six feet of Delaney and told him to jump toward us, as we couldn't get any nearer him, the wind was blowing us back and it was getting colder. He wouldn't jump, he said he was too cold and he couldn't swim and he was afraid to jump and he drifted away from us..."

# CHAPTER FOUR

The necktie is a curious part of a salesman's wardrobe. That fancy piece of knotted fabric serves little purpose, save to hide missing collar buttons and to catch wayward drops of stew.

Joseph Harper, however, was one man who found value in his businessman's tie. When the *Mayflower* went down, a soaking wet cravat was Harper's tenuous grip on life.

Imlach, O'Brien, Harper and Peverly drifted in the frigid waters of Lake Kamaniskeg. Parcher had swum off to shore, the rest had quickly drowned. They were alone. The rough box containing the coffin and Brown's body served as their life-ring. It saved them from drowning, but offered no protection from the relentless wind and the heartlessly numbing cold lake.

"I could discern the north shore about one hundred yards away, the wind increased considerably. Imlach caught a hold of Mr. O'Brien to help him keep his hold on the coffin," is how Gordon Peverly retold the story to the *Toronto Star*. Even though they could see land, the wind and the current took them out towards the open lake.

"We drifted for quite a considerable time and Imlach held onto O'Brien who got delirious and seemed to lose his head altogether. Mr. Harper and I got a hold of the other end of the rough box," recalled Peverly. "For three hours we drifted with the wind (away from land) I could see the dim outline of what looked like a tree a short distance away."

According to Peverly, the box drifted up to the floating tree. The men were able to steady the coffin against the trunk of the deadhead while Peverly climbed up onto the log and onto the top of the coffin. He took off his shoes and prepared to go back into the chilling waters of the lake — it was easier to swim without heavy boots, despite the fact that his toes quickly froze.

Peverly climbed off the pine box into the water. He kicked away the log and the men once again began to drift farther away from rescue. A few minutes after the tree disappeared from sight into the inky night, Harper gasped out; he didn't think he could keep a hold of the coffin any longer. It was then that Peverly remembered his business-suit tie.

"Knowing I was the only one who could swim, with one hand I pulled off my necktie. I gave one end to Harper and keeping hold of the other I struck out for shore (or rather where Peverly thought the shore should be) pulling the coffin. The three men clung to the coffin and kicked with their feet as best they could.

"We kept on swimming till Mr. Harper said he felt bottom. And soon I felt bottom too. But it was a rock and we got into deep water again," continued Peverly.

The elation of finding land and then losing it again was shattering. Luckily the torture was short-lived. The survivors reckoned that ten minutes later the coffin and four men reached the rocky, slippery, shallow shores of a small island.

"Harper and I got there," continued Peverly. "And I got the necktie off my wrist and went back to help O'Brien (who was being held by Imlach by this time)."

John Imlach was with O'Brien throughout the night, they shared the same side of the coffin. He knew that Paddy O'Brien was in trouble. "During the several hours we were in the water we (Imlach and O'Brien) slapped each other's faces and bodies to keep ourselves sensible, the cold was so intense," said Imlach.

"I waded back and I got my arms under his (O'Brien's) and walked backwards and we got to the shore," said Peverly, taking up the story where Imlach left off. "I was sitting down in shallow water when Mr. O'Brien threw back his head and I heard the gurgle in his throat and he was gone."

Patrick "Paddy" O'Brien was dead. The fifty-nine-year-old owner of the O'Brien House had died of exposure. His grieving widow and four grown children were told that his last words to his wife were: "Tell Tillie goodbye."

Paddy had lived in Radcliffe Township since 1874. He was a self-made man, the deed to his 4th Concession property is without signature, O'Brien used an X as his mark. Along with his hotel he also ran the village's first private phone

**Mr. and Mrs. Paddy O'Brien sit on the front porch of their Combermere hotel.**

Photograph – Jean Richter Collection

company, which accounted for the almost total news black-out that followed the recovery of his body. His family and staff went into mourning, closing down the village's switchboard. Reporters for the Ottawa papers ended up interviewing the conductor from the GTR train to get information about the disaster.

The body of O'Brien was dragged onto the flat bank of the tiny island. The three survivors went back into the water and retrieved the box carrying Brown's body. In death he had saved their lives, they weren't about to let his body simply float away.

O'Brien's body was placed in a snow-drift and the three travellers huddled beside the coffin. The water ordeal had been survived, now began the agony of the frozen night.

**The O'Brien Hotel in Combermere still stands today. After the death of Paddy O'Brien the building changed hands and uses several times. It is currently used as a clothing bank by St. Joseph's Church.**

Photograph — S. Weir

"Imlach was the first one to realize we would have to have some better shelter and he went over and got us shelter by a large stone," remembered Gordon Peverly. "Well, we stayed in the shelter of this large stone till morning."

By this time Harper had very sore, frost-bitten feet. His boots, discarded in the lake, were missed. Shortly after making landfall, the Ottawa shoe salesman could stand it no longer... "When O'Brien died I took his boots off and put them on myself."

The night passed with a deadly slowness. The three men, huddling beside a coffin and the body of a frozen companion, fought off the wind and a growing snowstorm. In the morning they paced the rocky island's shore line, scanning the waters for a sign of rescue. There was little to see, but the walking kept them alive.

"About the next morning, another boat, the *Ruby* went up and we tried to make her see us or hear us, but she went right ahead, and she came back about noon but we didn't see her," said Peverly when testifying to a government commission investigating the loss of the *Mayflower*. "She (the *Ruby*) went down on the other side of the island and we didn't see her. She came up again about three o'clock in the afternoon and we couldn't make her see us. Then we decided, after she passed the third time, that we had to get a fire..."

Harper saved the day. He remembered getting a gas lighter from Hudson just before the *Mayflower* sank. In those days, lighters were curios rather than functional items of smoking paraphernalia. Harper searched his pockets but the lighter wasn't in any of them.

The three Lake Kamaniskeg Robinson Crusoes, with little else to do, searched the water's edge for the souvenir fire starter. For once the men's lucky star twinkled brightly —

they found the lighter on the shore in a snowbank. Huddling around the thing, it took what seemed like an hour to blow dry its long string wick. When a flame was finally struck, a fire was started using *Mayflower* jetsom.

Harper had been badly affected by his ordeal. His thought patterns were jumbled, he was not thinking clearly. Stranded, soaking wet on an island in the midst of a late-fall snowstorm, it took the Ottawa salesman almost a day to remember that he had one of those newfangled lighters in his pocket.

Even at the inquest, a month later, Harper was in a bad state both physically and mentally. He was asked at the hearing why he had trouble walking. The following quote is verbatim from the lips of Mr. Harper:

"It is a combination of a freeze and a burn, I think." said Harper pointing at a bound foot. "It (the foot) was freezing before we got the fire started, and, then I got my foot in the fire (to warm it) — hence the burn."

It was after Harper burned his foot in the fire that the survivors began to give up hope.

"We realized that we would have to spend another night there," said Peverly. "My spirits went very low. We gathered some wood to keep up the fire and we had two empty boxes that came out of the water. I sat in one and the other two boys sat against the other, with one overcoat, and we stayed in that position until we heard the boat whistling. I should judge it about nine o'clock in the evening and we waved a burning branch to them and they whistled right back..."

The horror was over.

Above top, the coffin drifted to the shore of Parcher Island, named after Aaron Parcher, a victim of the *Mayflower* tragedy.
Above, the wreck of the *Mayflower* lies on the bottom of Lake Kamaniskeg near Parcher Island. Three survivors of the *Mayflower* spent a night on this island.

# CHAPTER FIVE

Andy Imlach knew two things with a certainty that, unlike the *Mayflower*, was unsinkable. He laughed at the thought that something as trivial as a shipwreck could kill his brother, John Imlach. However, he also believed that the news of the loss of the ship would be the death of their dear mother.

J. S. Imlach was twenty-nine years of age when he survived the November sinking of the paddle-wheel ship. The General Supply Company traveller was considered, at least by Ottawa's *The Evening Journal*, to be one of the city's most popular bachelors. He lived in an apartment at his parents' home on Thornton Street in the capital city. The 1912 voyage was the first long trip away from home that he took for the company.

Mr. and Mrs. Andrew Imlach were principal owners of the Victoria Foundry Company. Young Andy Imlach was employed by Victoria Garage Company, an offshoot of his father's business.

When Andy Jr. learned that the *Mayflower* had gone down and that his brother was missing and presumed drowned, he left his job at a dead run. Grabbing a knife from a tool bench near the shop's door, Andy raced for the back of his parents' house. When he reached it, he took out his blade and sliced through the telephone wire that led into the family home.

He explained later to his brother that he had cut the wires so that no news could come through to his mother until he was certain of his brother's fate.

Andy kept his mother entertained with stories and local gossip for two hours. She said later that she was sure her son had been "unexpectedly successful at work, he was that high-spirited."

When John Imlach was finally brought to shore aboard the *Ruby*, he immediately thought of his mother. When his phone calls failed to ring through (thanks to his brother 's knife) he called a neighbour who walked over to the Imlach house and told the family that John was safe. That was the first inkling the Imlach seniors had of John's brush with a fresh-water Davy Jones.

John's call was placed from the O'Brien Hotel, the inn owned by Imlach's coffin mate, Paddy O'Brien. It might seem odd that the survivors would impose themselves on the grief-stricken owners and staff of the O'Brien. But they didn't have much choice, the other hotel in town was owned by the Hudsons.

When the three survivors had notified their relatives of the rescue and fielded a very few calls from reporters, the O'Brien family shut down the switchboard. The O'Briens, like the rest of the village, went into mourning in honour of Paddy and the others lost in the November mishap.

This self-imposed black-out caused the newspapers no end of trouble. The stories that were initially printed were very garbled. Much of the misinformation that has been printed about the *Mayflower* can probably be traced back to those few initial, erroneous reports.

The Ottawa papers quoted a railroad conductor while the *Toronto Star*, drawing on unidentified sources, called the captain by the name of Parker (probably referring to the pilot, Parcher) and had the *Mayflower* sinking three miles out of Barry's Bay with both Hudson brothers on board.

An Ottawa newspaper and a valley weekly placed the old woman, Mrs. William McWhirter, out on the lake aboard the floating coffin. One paper even went so far as to say that the men on the coffin cut her loose when she started to struggle in the water.

The two Pembroke papers, scooped by their big-city rivals, neglected to inform readers about the mishap.

Meanwhile papers all across North America were running *Mayflower* items. The following is part of an article that appeared in the *Dayton Ohio Daily News*, dated November 14, 1912. It is indicative of the coverage that papers gave the disaster.

# Eleven Perish In The River

*Eleven persons probably perished when the steamboat* **Mayflower** *sank in the Madawaska River, read a dispatch today from Barry's Bay, three miles from the scene of the disaster... the three survivors are so weak that they can tell little about how the accident occurred. They were found last night half-frozen on an island three miles below where the boat sank. A search party has found only two bodies. A snowstorm raged last night and this morning.*

The two bodies mentioned in the Dayton clipping were those of Paddy O'Brien and Parcher the pilot. It took the efforts of a local MP to muster the professional help needed to find all but one of the remaining *Mayflower* victims.

Gerald Verner White was a thirty-three-year-old valley politician whose roots were solidly planted in the Barry's Bay/Pembroke communities. He was a director of the

Pembroke Lumber Company and a five-year Conservative member sitting for Renfrew North.

Gerald White, like his father Peter (who held the riding until his retirement in 1908), was a quiet man in the House of Commons. According to *Hansard*, in 1912 he spoke only twice in Parliament and on both occasions he managed to say his piece in fewer than five sentences.

Despite his reticence in formal debates, White was a seasoned politician who was loyal to his riding. He knew the power that a back-bencher in Robert Borden's Tory government could call upon in times of need.

The Combermere search team, led by Jack's brother Hal Hudson, found two bodies. By Friday, November 15, Robert Pachal, the Yorkton, Saskatchewan farmer who had brought the coffin to the *Mayflower*, was found floating near the island where the Ottawa travellers had landed. The body of the fireman, Tom Delaney, was found near the wreck of the *Mayflower*.

**North Renfrew Conservative MP Gerald V. White sounded the call for action when news of the sinking of the *Mayflower* reached him in Pembroke. At his urging, government divers were sent to Lake Kamaniskeg to look for the bodies of those who died in the mishap.**

Photograph — Pembroke — Canada's Next City, published 1915, Pembroke.

The local searchers figured that the rest of the bodies were to be found inside the wreck. With this fact in hand, Gerald White went into action. In a telegram dated November 15, 1912, White called on James Hunter, the Deputy Minister of Public Works, to arrange to "send a diver to Barry's Bay tomorrow, Saturday morning. *Mayflower* found. Several bodies known to be in cabin of boat."

Hunter didn't have any divers to send. But the Minister of Marine and Fisheries, at White's urging, did. After receiving a copy of the White cable, he dispatched a hard-hat diver from Smiths Falls to the wreck site. James Scott arrived in Combermere on Sunday, November 17.

Scott was taken out to the *Mayflower*, probably by the *Ruby*. There was no trouble in finding her, the flag-pole served as a marker and an anchor post.

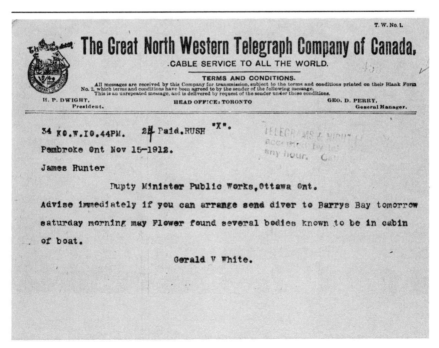

**A copy of the telegraph that was sent by MP Gerald White calling for divers to assist in the search for bodies. The telegram brought immediate action.**

After getting into his heavy boots, canvas suit and brass helmet, Scott was lowered into the water. He soon stood on top of the sunken ship.

The weight of the diver's equipment was such that Scott walked rather than swam about the *Mayflower*. A pump on board the *Ruby* fed air to the man below.

"I went down on the boat and I had to walk to one end of it to see which was the bow or stern," said Scott twelve days after that first dive.

"I went to the stern and by the paper I had, they said (*sic*) I would find the most of the bodies in the cabin. I walked up to the bow and got down — jumped down onto her deck — and walked up around her bow and I got one man lying inside the rail, I don't know who he was. I didn't know any of them."

**An unidentified government diver is being prepared to make a dive into the Madawaska River. The photograph was taken at Madawaska Point c. 1895-1915.**

Photograph — The Ontario Archives 4212-5934

"I went into the cabin and I got the body of an old lady in there floating around. Then I took the old lady out on the bow, to the part that wasn't enclosed and I tied the two bodies together... and they were hauled up."

Scott made another circuit of the *Mayflower* and then dropped down onto the sandy bottom and walked around the perimeter of the upright wreck. He continued to find corpses but there was still one body missing. He did his best to find it.

On the deck of the tender ship, the identification of the diver's catch began. There was Mrs. William McWhirter, the Combermere tailor William Boehme, Rockingham resident William Murphy and the owner of the ship John Hudson. True to his ship, Hudson had stayed with her to the end.

The body of George Bothwell could not be found. The twenty-seven-year-old salesman for the Ottawa produce firm of F. J. Castle & Co. jumped through the open section of the ship's door just as she began to take on water. The Nepean Street resident was described by friends as "an ace swimmer of splendid physique." It was possible that Bothwell tried to swim for shore and drowned before reaching land.

The searchers knew that if Bothwell's body had entered the current of the Madawaska River they would have a devil of a time finding him. There are thirty-eight miles of navigable waters near Combermere and the Madawaska River itself is the largest south-bank tributary in the Ottawa Valley. From its source, north of Lake Kamaniskeg, down to Arnprior, where it joins the Ottawa River, the Madawaska runs for two hundred miles.

On Monday, November 18, Scott went back into the water to examine the wreck and to continue the hunt for

Bothwell. He found no trace of the man. He made a third dive on the nineteenth, but again Bothwell's body wasn't to be found.

Long before the searchers gave up looking for Bothwell's body, his friends knew that all was lost. On November 15, a notice was put in the paper by Mr. H. Chamberlain, the president of the Castle Company, mourning the loss of a valued employee.

In Ottawa, MP White continued to express his concerns about the loss of the *Mayflower*. Hazen, the Minister of Marines and Fisheries, was quick to act. He announced, even before the valley men had quit dragging the lake and the river, there would be a government investigation and hearing into the sinking of the *Mayflower*.

On the twentieth of November, Mr. R. A. Pringle KC, an Ottawa barrister with the firm Pringle, Thompson and Burgess, was picked to head the investigation. He left immediately for Combermere where he joined diver Scott out on the lake.

Pringle and Scott stayed in Combermere for three more days. Leaving the search for Bothwell in the hands of Dr. Poirer of Craigmont and Stephen Smith, a carpenter and undertaker from Barry's Bay, Pringle left for Ottawa to begin a formal hearing into the loss of the ship. With the first witness appearing on November 29, 1912, the hearing began less than three weeks after the ship sank and ended months before the body of Bothwell was finally found.

# CHAPTER SIX

It took just four days of public hearings to tar and feather the dead shipowner's reputation. Jack Hudson was being mourned by the citizens of Combermere when the official inquiry began to sit in Ottawa. When Justice Pringle handed down his findings to the Minister of Marine and Fisheries, the captain's good name had sunk lower into the mud than the ill-fated *Mayflower*.

When the hearing started, Hudson was still considered a hard-working steamship owner, a man who tried to save his lake stern-wheeler at the expense of his own life. People talked of his commitment to the community: he was the reeve of Radcliffe Township, he owned a sawmill and operated, with his mother and brother, a large hotel. Once the report was released to the press, front-page stories across the country branded him as irresponsible, a drunkard and a law-breaker.

It was a nasty hearing. Not only was Hudson's name besmirched along the way, but one of the key witnesses at the wreck inquiry, a government hull inspector, was censured by the justice member for not grounding the *Mayflower* at the beginning of the 1912 shipping season. So severe was the criticism, the civil servant considered suing the lawyer who sat at the head of the Bench.

As each day of the Ottawa hearing progressed, strip upon strip was taken off Hudson's good name. Witness after witness gave damning testimony about the conduct of the *Mayflower* owner and the newspapers dutifully carried items relaying same. Jack would have fared better if he'd been keel-hauled under his own stern-wheel paddler.

In fact, in one way, the tarnishing of Jack Hudson's name began even before Robert Pringle was appointed hearing commissioner. An anonymous letter, date-lined Toronto November 13, 1912 (the day after the sinking), was received by the Minister of Marine and Fisheries. It was used as evidence at the inquiry even though it offered no proof as to the serious charges it leveled against Hudson.

The note reads as follows, without grammatical adjustments:

**Re "STR *Mayflower*".**

*In connection with the loss of life entailed by sinking of the above boat, the writer believes the following to facts.*

*The boat sank during season of 1911 and was raised by a few temporary repairs made. She had no qualified master or engineer, the owner who was among the lost has not been known to have been sober for twelve months. He was acting Engineer and Captain, and a youth about 18 years of age was wheelman. They charge $1.50 for a trip of twelve miles. No fire appliances or pails. On looking for inspection certificate could seen none but one of 1910. The disaster anticipated by many who knew the conditions. I think a full report should be obtained from Steamboat Inspector for that district.*

*Yours very truly,*

*Observer*

33435 NOV 16 1912

Toronto, November 13th, 1912.

Minister of Marine,

Ottawa, Ontario.

My dear Sir :-

Re "STR. MAYFLOWER".

In connection with the loss of life entailed by sinking of the above boat, the writer believes the following to be facts.

The boat sank during season of 1911, and was raised by a few temporary repairs made. She had no qualified master or engineer; the owner who was among the lost has not been known to have been sober for twelve months. He was acting Engineer and Captain, and a youth about 18 years of age was wheelman. They charged $1.50 for a trip of twelve miles. No fire appliances or pails. On looking for inspection certificate could see none but one of 1910. The disaster was anticipated by many who knew the conditions. I think a full report should be obtained from Steamboat Inspector for that District.

Yours very truly,

Observer.

**John Hudson had his detractors. The above anonymous letter was sent to the federal government after the *Mayflower* sank. It accuses the boat owner of drunkenness.**

Canadian Archives — RG 42 Volume 1784

The identity of the mysterious 'Observer' was never discovered. Despite the writer's lack of backbone when it came time to sign his letter, the Minister of Marine and Fisheries took the charges seriously. Certain claims in the note rang true — she was travelling without a certificate and yes, the *Mayflower* had sunk the year before. However, an inspection in the fall noted proper safety equipment, including life-jackets and pails. As for the charge of imbibing, it could well be true that Hudson was a heavy drinker. However, the fervour of prohibition was hitting the valley with a vengeance, the town of Renfrew had gone dry in about 1911 and one must consider the temper, or should one say temperance, of the times when considering those salacious remarks.

The cast of characters who took part in the formal drama of the hearing illustrate, through the testimony they gave, the four different questions that the investigators addressed.

Why did the *Mayflower* sink? Why did the government allow the ship to operate without a captain on board? What caused the passengers to perish? And, the final question that was pondered at the Ottawa hearing was, of course, what sort of man was Jack Hudson?

A cross-section of people from Combermere came forward to give testimony. Three survivors gave evidence and a number of government inspectors were grilled on the stand.

## What Caused The Mayflower To Sink?

A quick off-the-cuff remark on the part of a Barry's Bay town official a day after the sinking was the most popular reason cited in the papers as to the cause of the *Mayflower's* demise. However, after the wreck inquest was held, it turned out that the initial guess was just that, and it was many nautical miles off target.

"Steamer Leaking Before She Left Wharf Is Latest Report" or so said the wire-service story that was run by scores of papers November 14, 1912. The reporter writing that release quoted an unidentified town employee as blaming the sinking on a leak that was sustained earlier in the day when the *Mayflower* bumped into the *Ruby* at the Barry's Bay dock, the afternoon of November 12.

The theory was put forward that the *Mayflower* had sustained more damage than any member of the crew had realized, and, while traveling back to Combermere that night, the damaged hull of the *Mayflower* simply caved in, sinking the freighter with only seconds warning.

The three men who survived the wreck readily told reporters and anyone else who would listen that when they were on the *Mayflower* her syphon pump was running, indicating that water was getting into the ship somehow. However, testimony at the hearing soon proved that the leaking theory leaked.

Henry Leach, the Ottawa salesman who was on board the *Mayflower* when it hit the *Ruby*, described the accident in detail. His observations made it seem highly unlikely that the afternoon accident could have caused the evening disaster.

"When we came into the wharf some man on the deck of the *Ruby*, near the stern, caught the bow of the boat we were on to avoid a crash. For some reason, I don't know what, we seemed to strike the *Ruby* but she did not collide with any force, there was no cause for alarm. I was standing with my hand on the rail and the jar was not sufficient to cause me to lose my balance. We did not strike heavily."

W. M. Martin, a Barry's Bay resident, was on the dock with his team of horses when the wooden *Mayflower* struck the steamer *Ruby*. After glancing off the docked steamer the *Mayflower* docked with ease, and, according to Martin, didn't have enough speed up to hit the pilings after the initial collision. Dougall Gates, the captain of the *Ruby*, agreed with Martin. Captain Gates did not see the *Mayflower* hit the wharf after glancing off the side of his tug.

When asked if the *Mayflower* had the appearance then (the afternoon of November 12, 1912) of being loaded down with water, Captain Gates answered, "No, she never looked any different to me from what she always did."

**The Hudson brothers put their partnership into writing before the *Mayflower* sailed. There is no record of their partnership being formally broken, although Hal Hudson did testify at the *Mayflower* inquest that he had sold his share of the business to his brother John. (And John's widow wrote that she had sold the rights of the ship back to Hal after the wreck).**

Canadian Archives RG 42 Volume 1784

Jack Hudson's brother, Henry Edward Hudson, explained away the use of the *Mayflower's* syphon. Jack and Henry had a fifty/fifty ownership of the *Mayflower* until 1907 and Henry had crewed on the vessel until a month before her final sinking. The Barry's Bay resident said it was standard practice to have the vessel's pump running to remove water from her slight hull.

Could the *Mayflower* have been damaged sometime before her last day of operation? Apparently not. According to Hudson's brother, the ship had stood at the dock overnight (November 11) without sinking, even though she was loaded down with twelve tons of freight and no pump was running. Henry Hudson felt this was evidence enough that the *Mayflower* was sturdy and seaworthy.

If the mild, pier-side knock-up was not the cause of the ship's death, and a leaky hull was not at fault, what was the final straw that pulled the plug on Jack Hudson's shipping business? For an answer to that, one has to go underwater.

James Scott, the Ottawa diver, testified early in the inquiry that he had removed the bodies of the victims trapped underwater in the wreck of the *Mayflower*. Scott told the hearing that once he had helped haul the dead up to the surface of the lake he returned underwater to the ship and retrieved the luggage. After that he, and later another government diver, closely examined the hull of the stern-wheeler to see exactly why she had sunk.[6]

"I went all around the hull outside, I had a brace and bit and I bored holes in twenty-five or thirty places along the hull," testified the government diver at the inquest.

[6] *Scott received $146.00 for his work.*

The results of the test borings jived with the testimony given at the hearing by the Combermere villagers who helped build the wooden ship — she was built with top-grade materials. Hudson owned a lumber-yard and had used only the best in the construction of his ship. "I found it sound, every hole I bored, except when I bored near a bolt or a spike and the wood would be blackened, indicating the beginning signs of rot," continued Scott.

Scott wore a helmet of brass on top of a watertight suit of canvas. Heavily leaded boots kept him on the bottom. A pump on board the *Ruby* supplied him with a steady stream of compressed air. The hard-hat diver had no

**This diver is laying a ball-joint pipe across the Madawaska River. The gear that he is wearing was standard issue in the early 1900s and is indicative of what divers wore when they searched for the victims of the *Mayflower* sinking. The identity of the diver is not known, but he could be one of two government-directed *Mayflower* divers who recovered bodies and investigated the wreck of the *Mayflower*. This photograph was taken c. 1895-1915.**

Photograph — Ontario Archives 3026-54872

difficulty staying underwater long enough to complete a very thorough study of the vessel.

Scott found that the oak used in the construction of the hull was in a perfect state.[7] However, the planks themselves were not tightly fitted together. James Scott said he didn't find any open seams, "but, I found the oak kind of loose, I could get hold of the screw on the boat and pull it out."

It took the work of Scott's diving partner, Benoit Rouleau, to find the terminal weakness of the *Mayflower*. Rouleau, a Smiths Falls resident, was a diver working for the City of Ottawa. He and Scott were drafted from their different underwater jobs and teamed together by the federal government at the request of the warden of Renfrew County and the Department of Railways and Canals. Scott, the senior diver of the team, worked for the department.

With a hammer and a chisel, Rouleau took wood samples wherever he suspected weak lumber. His samples of pine and oak, entered as evidence at the hearing, backed Scott's early statements. Both types of wood found in the ship's hull were in A-one condition.

No, the problem was not with the wood, it was with the oakum. Oakum is a caulking material, usually made from tarred frayed-rope fibres, that is used to seal the seams in a ship's hull. Since the boards in a boat's hull can't be placed so tightly together that they make the vessel watertight, oakum is used to get the job done. Before a ship is launched in the spring, the oakum is jammed between the boards to seal the hull and keep the insides of the boat dry.

[7] *Scuba divers will find that close to eighty years later the oak hull is still in surprisingly good shape.*

"I examined the boat all around while underwater and I saw some oakum that was loose, there was a broken window there and I got a piece of glass from the wreckage to see if I could put it through the boards," said Benoit Rouleau. "I took that piece of glass and it went right through."

The disintegration of the oakum came as a shocking surprise to people who knew the history of the *Mayflower*. She had sunk the year before and Hudson, upon raising her, decided the seams should be examined.

He called upon John Waddington, relative, friend, next-door neighbour and at one time an employee of the Hudson brothers, to look at the hull. Waddington spoke at the hearing about the overhaul work he did on the ship in the spring of 1912. "There were some seams in the stern that were caulked again and we repainted it and done all that was necessary (*sic*)."

"Then you found loose seams?" Waddington was quizzed. "Well they wasn't loose (*sic*) but we could put some more caulking in and we did it."

Hudson didn't spare any expense with the ship's wood and there was no reason for him to skimp on the other raw materials used in the repair of his beloved *Mayflower*.

Jeremiah Connelly had a sawmill in Combermere, he planed the wood used in the *Mayflower's* construction. Connelly was willing to swear to the high quality of the wood that Hudson brought to his yard for planing. It is unthinkable that the oakum would have been anything other than top of the line.

The oakum came loose not because it was cheap oakum, but rather because of the ship's design and the modifications that Hudson made to that design.

As the testimony at the inquest indicated, there had been adjustments made to the wood in the paddle-wheel at the back of the *Mayflower*. Hudson had customized the slats of wood that protruded, at regular intervals, from the water-wheel. These cross-beams, or buckets, dug deep into the water and propelled the ship forward. Since the *Mayflower* travelled in shallow waters, Hudson had modified the buckets to reduce their depth — he didn't want the buckets scraping the bottom and possibly breaking off.

It isn't recorded in the inspection reports as to when those modifications took place. However, according to testimony at the hearing, the government inspectors who looked over the ship each year remembered seeing the adjusted buckets in the spring of 1912. And while the design of the *Mayflower* might well have been sound, the additional changes to the ship's water-wheel were ultimately responsible for taking those passengers to their cold water demise.

"I am of the opinion that certain changes having been made to the paddles, the effect was to place a greater strain on that boat, and there being a fairly heavy wind on the night of the twelfth of November 1912, the strain was increased and the seams were opened in that portion of the hull near the paddle where the water rushed in very rapidly, and before anyone on board noticed the water, the stern was practically submerged," wrote Justice Pringle in his final report to the federal cabinet.

"It was a sudden filling up, as otherwise it would have affected the fire in the *Mayflower's* boiler." The report continued, "According to the evidence the water was not noticed until it was rushing in over the deck at both sides of the boat where there were openings."

Now, the *Bluenose* is the sort of ship that a stay-at-home hobbyist might want to miniaturize and painstakingly rebuild inside a small clear glass bottle. Her shape is a harmony of art and classic maritime engineering.

And then there is the *Mayflower*.

Quite simply, the *Mayflower* was an ugly boat. Collectors will never see her profile on the backside of a dime or on the face of a Canadian stamp. She was built crudely for functional reasons. No thoughts were given to the comfort of the passengers, Hudson cared little what people thought when they saw the *Mayflower* tied up at the dock.

The boat looked like a pioneer-style frame house roughly placed atop a flat-bottomed hull. At the bow of the boat there was an almost straight flag-pole, at midship a sooty smoke-stack saluted the sky and out of a gash at the square-backed stern of the ship was a churning water-wheel.

While this unpleasant looking lake steamer was not about to win any maritime dressage championships, there was sound purpose to the way in which the designer, Montreal boat builder J. R. Weir, had drawn up her blueprints.

She was built stern-heavy on a nearly flat bottom, so that there was very little of her sitting below the water-line.

"There is an engine on each side of the boat and they extend back to the shaft, I should say about ten feet from the stern of the boat. The shaft would revolve on the engine bearing," testified Napoleon Tessier, the boat builder, at the inquest held to look into the events surrounding the loss of the ship. Tessier followed Weir's instructions as he installed, with the Hudsons' help, the engines into the *Mayflower's* hull back in 1902. Fittingly, Tessier lived in the city of Hull, Quebec.

The *Mayflower*, when fully loaded, carried its cargo in the bow to balance the weight of the engines and wheel in the stern. The end result was that the ship could skim across the water.

This made the *Mayflower* damnably hard to keep on course. Since there was little of her in the water to act as a keel, the slightest wind blew the freighter off course. Hudson avoided sailing into a strong wind because a healthy blow could push the *Mayflower* backwards, even when the furnace was fully stoked and the boiler had a full head of steam.

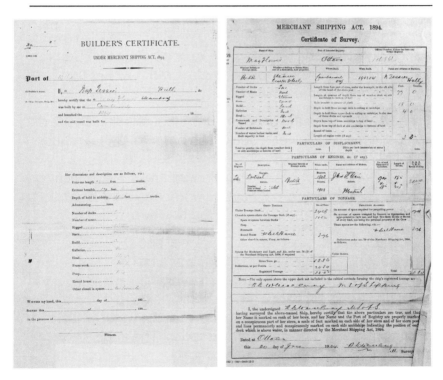

Above left, the *Mayflower's* Builder's Certificate was signed by Napoleon Tessier.
Above right, the *Mayflower's* Certificate of Survey was completed in June of 1904.

Canadian Archives RG 42 Volume 1784

The failings of the *Mayflower* in breezy conditions were compensated for by her ability to travel in the shallowest of waters. Even when she was fully loaded, the *Mayflower* could sail in two and one-half feet of water — that is only about twice the depth of a bath-tub.

Back at the turn of the century, Lake Kamaniskeg was not the controlled body of water it is today. Sand-bars jammed portions of both the lake and the Madawaska River and, when the levels were low, the Narrows were too shallow even for the likes of the *Mayflower*. The sand-bars were often dredged to allow the *Mayflower*, the *Tiger* and the *Ruby* safe passage and to ensure a steady flow of goods and services between the railroad station in Barry's Bay and the corundum mines of Craigmont where thirteen hundred men worked in 1912.

Even with the constant dredging, the Hudsons had decided to modify the *Mayflower's* buckets in order to further reduce the draft of the vessel. By shortening the blades the *Mayflower* could travel just about anywhere in the district and the captain would not have to worry about the ever-changing depth of the sand near the Narrows.

Jack Hudson's brother was an engineer and probably designed the changes to the *Mayflower's* blades. At the inquest, he explained just how the stern wheel was adjusted. Using his hands, he gestured as he told how every second paddle was removed from the water-wheel and the remaining blades were turned in. The angle of attack for the bucket blade was no longer ninety degrees — the modified slats now gently kissed the water rather than dug into it.

"It was so the paddle would roll in the water all the time instead of hitting the water," explained the younger Hudson brother.

Henry's comment was made long before the phrase 'rock and roll ' was coined. So it was without humour that he said the changes in the *Mayflower's* paddles made a "difference, there was a kind of rocking all the time instead of a regular roll."

The ship was stern-heavy on her last voyage, there were only thirteen people on board, counting both the living and the dead, and there was no cargo in her hold. There was not nearly enough weight to properly balance out the steamer. The unbalanced boat, the strong wind, the adjusted paddles and the weakened oakum combined to cause the sinking of the ship.

This is how the federal inquiry chairman, Justice Pringle called it: "I am of the opinion that certain changes having been made in the paddles the effect was to place a greater strain on the boat, and there being a fairly heavy wind on the night of the twelfth of November 1912, the strain was increased and the seams were opened in that portion of the hull near the paddle-wheel where the water rushed in very rapidly, as before anyone on board noticed the water, the stern was practically submerged.

"It was a sudden filling up as otherwise the fireman would have noticed the water as it would have affected the fire that fed the boiler," wrote Robert Pringle in his final statement to the federal cabinet. "According to the evidence, the water was not noticed until it was rushing in over the deck at both sides of the boat where there were openings, I should say the middle of the boat."

# Why Was There No Captain On Board That Night?

The owner of the *Mayflower* went down with his ship. While that is an honour usually reserved for the captain, in

1912's shipping season, the *Mayflower* had no legal captain on board. Hudson was a suitable substitute.

In this day and age of strict government regulations on all aspects of transportation, it seems extremely odd that a passenger-carrying vessel could operate for a complete season without proper papers and without a certified master on board. What makes it even more unbelievable was that this could happen a year after the *Mayflower* sank in the Madawaska River with paying customers aboard. But that is precisely what happened; the lack of certification was the norm for ships operating in that era.

The early 1900s were years of change for the inland maritime shipping industry. More and more vessels were being built with engines, displacing the sailing-ship as the favoured mode of lake travel. The increase in powered craft outstripped the number of available government inspectors who were supposed to certify all ships before the start of each shipping year.

Under the federal government's Department of Marine and Fisheries regulations, shipowners needed two separate certifications from federal inspectors each spring before a ship was licensed to take passengers and freight. The hull inspector closely examined every commercial vessel in the country. He was looking at every aspect of the ship's construction. The government wanted to be sure that before a boat got into the water its hull was proven to be seaworthy. The inspection sheet used by the federal employee listed everything from the quality and dimension of the timber used in the hull right down to the number of lights and fog bells used by the ship when in operation.

The engine inspector, on the other hand, was concerned with the condition of the ship's power plant, and he would visit fleet owners to examine the engines and the boilers.

He didn't care about the crew or their training, save for the fact that he would always ask to see the captain's papers.

The two inspectors did not travel together. Since not all commercial carriers had engines, there were more ships for the hull inspector to inspect than the engine inspector. As a result, the hull inspector was assigned a much smaller territory. The *Mayflower's* engine was given the official once-over on August 28, three full months after the hull inspector had come to pay his professional respects.

A favourable report from both inspectors was needed before the steamer could legally carry paying passengers. Since in those days shipowners had to wait months before receiving the necessary papers, it was common practice for boats to travel under the previous year's certification slip.

That all-important piece of paper, when finally issued, was called the coasting licence. It was issued by the customs department rather than the department of Marine and Fisheries, even though the inspections were carried out by Marine employees. And it was up to the customs department, and not the fisheries people, to enforce the licensing of the steamer — an unwieldy arrangement since it was the inspectors who were in a position to spot violators.

M. R. Davis, the hull inspector who looked at the *Mayflower*, explained the bureaucratic entanglement at the hearing thusly:

"The trouble is here, Mr. Pringle. I am the Inspector of Hulls and Equipment for two districts, Mr. Laurie (the boiler inspector who had certified the *Mayflower's* power plant) belongs to the Montreal district and I belong to the Kingston District or the Eastern Ontario District. A Mr. Thompson inspects the machinery in the Kingston district and I inspect the hull and equipment for steamers in both districts, and that requires me to travel a long distance from home, and for that reason, in the spring of the year when the shipping is starting, there are a great many inspections at the front of the season, at home in Kingston and the near vicinity requiring our constant service in the neighbourhood of six weeks. While the inspections are going on outside, by Mr. Laurie, I cannot give them my attention and boats that he may inspect in the district I cover in April, he may not inspect until August.

"The boating is increasing in the back lakes of Ontario all the time causing a wider inspection area, therefore you can fancy me going from Kingston to Porcupine and in that neighbourhood which is nearly seven hundred miles away," concluded Mr. Davis.

Be that as it may, Justice Pringle wasn't convinced that the government inspector was unaware of the fact that Hudson was running his passenger-ship operation without proper accreditation.

When Davis examined the *Mayflower* on May 28 he okayed every aspect of her, except for the little matter of her not having a licensed captain at the helm. Davis, in writing, advised Jack Hudson to stop carrying passengers until he could find a real master.

Davis went so far as to ask the helmsman who worked the *Mayflower* in 1911, a Captain McGlade, to return to the *Mayflower*. According to the letter sent to Jack Hudson by Davis, McGlade refused. The letter read in part:

"With reference to a Captain for your Steamer, beg to advise you it is impossible to find a man who will go. As I explained to you while there, you have no right to carry passengers until you have a proper Captain, and under the law, I am unable to issue you your Certificate.

"As Mr. Laurie the boiler inspector will no doubt be along in few days (sic) you better have him inspect your boat for a Tug Certificate, as that seems to be your only way for the present and drop the passenger business."

Jack Hudson, without a master on board, could transport freight and deliver the mail using a tugboat licence. According to the testimony of Inspector Davis, Hudson verbally agreed to this. Davis didn't pursue the matter any further. He told the hearing that he did not notify the customs department, which had the job of enforcing ships to live up to the letter of their licences, because he had no reason to doubt Hudson's word. If Jack Hudson said he wouldn't take passengers, Davis was quite willing to believe him.

Hudson wasn't above lying to government inspectors. When Mr. Laurie finally arrived in August to carry out his 1912 inspection, Hudson told him he did have a captain for the *Mayflower*.

"I found everything in a very good condition. The only fault there was to be found was that they had no Captain on board. And, Mr. Hudson told me then that the Captain had gone ashore sick, but he told me he would be back the next day and I told him to write me giving me the Captain's name and the number of his certificate as soon as he got back and he told me he would, and he done so," recalled Mr. Laurie.

Pringle then asked Laurie to name the man Hudson claimed was the captain. "McGlade, I think his name was. Peter, Peter McGlade," replied Mr. Laurie.

Peter McGlade had been the master of record in 1911, the year the *Mayflower* had first sunk. He left Hudson's employ after the accident and refused to return. That didn't stop Hudson from using his name and identification number.

To be fair to Hudson, the *Mayflower* was being run across a body of water that he knew better than any captain from outside the district. The ship charged $1.50 a trip per passenger and competition for freight between the *Mayflower*, the *Tiger* and the *Ruby* was fierce. More and more people were purchasing cars and the treacherous road was gradually being upgraded.

It is quite possible that Hudson simply couldn't afford to pay the going rate for a real captain. Considering his own problems — the *Mayflower* sinking in 1911 and the loss of the hotel by fire — one can understand why Hudson wouldn't be in a hurry to expand his payroll.

McGlade refused to go back to work for Hudson, his reasons unfortunately having been lost to time. Perhaps it was because Combermere was at the edge of the Ottawa Valley and wasn't considered a plum posting. As well, by 1912 the lumber cutters had moved on, there were no log booms moving through the Madawaska River — business would suffer and McGlade may have questioned the viability of the Hudson operation.

There were other good reasons for McGlade not to return to Lake Kamaniskeg. The *Mayflower* was a very hard ship to handle in a strong wind and the vessel had already sunk once. Hudson was a reputed drunk who ran a vessel in waters that were treacherous. McGlade had little reason to seriously consider working for Hudson again.

No mention is made in the records as to how much Hudson was willing to pay a registered captain. It is again speculation, but indications are that Hudson was a thrifty man. It could be that he was unwilling to pay the going rate.

An example of his frugality is well documented in the files of the Madawaska Improvement Company (MIC). The MIC was a consortium owned by Ottawa lumber barons and was concerned with the upkeep of dams and sluice-ways along the Madawaska River. The MIC made sure that log booms travelled from the wilds north of Lake Kamaniskeg down to the city of Ottawa.

The MIC owned a tug called the *Pioneer*. She was used to shepherd log booms from Bark Lake, the lake above Kamaniskeg, down through the Madawaska. She was built in 1888 at a cost of $5,900.00 and when she sank in Bark Lake in 1900, she was still valued at $1,000.00. Her upper deck remained out of the water and she was considered salvageable.

Hudson worked through MIC's agent, Thomas Dilon of Calabogie, to secure the salvage rights to the *Pioneer*. He wanted to raise the tug and examine her single engine to determine whether or not it was worth $100.00 − $900.00 less than the MIC wanted for her.

A company official, G. B. Greene, wrote that he would be 'ashamed' to take $100.00 under Hudson's conditions. He ordered that the boat be sold to Captain W. G. Jones, also of Combermere. Jones, a village store owner and boat captain, was willing to pay the same price as Hudson but was willing to take the wreck sight unseen.

Hudson lost the chance to buy the *Pioneer* because he wasn't willing to gamble the $100.00 needed to secure the undervalued wreck. The events of 1900 do, however, show that Jack Hudson was willing to work hard to put freighters into service on Lake Kamaniskeg, even to the point of raising the *Pioneer.*

# Why The Passengers Died

The Canadian government has always had broad shoulders. Since Confederation, the federal government has taken the blame for just about every major disaster that has occurred in the dominion. In 1912, the government took its share of the blame for the *Mayflower* deaths. When evidence was presented at the inquest showing that the hull inspector, M. E. Davis, was aware of the fact that Hudson was operating a passenger operation without a proper captain, Justice Pringle stated that Mr. Davis should have notified the customs department that, *ipso facto*, Hudson was in violation of the law. And further than that, Pringle declared that the *Mayflower* should have been seized by federal authorities.

The press was quick to play up the government-negligence angle. "Knowing the facts, Commissioner Pringle says Davis should have taken steps to seize and detain the vessel," read an article in the February 6, 1913, edition of the daily *Montreal Star*. "Davis took the ground that this was the duty of the Customs Department. But Mr. Pringle holds that the inspector should have informed the Customs Department of the gross violation of the law."

Inspector Davis went to his member of parliament in Kingston, Ontario to complain about the treatment he received at the hearing and in the newspapers. Mr. Nickle, the sitting member, wrote to the Honourable D. Hazen, the Minister in charge of Marine and Fisheries on behalf of Davis.

The rambling three-page letter makes reference to the many newspaper articles that reported Davis was aware of Hudson's disregard of the shipping laws. This is how Nickle, in part, defended the actions of Davis in this matter in a February 17, 1913, letter to Hazen.

"Mr. Davis tells me that on May 28th, 1912 he inspected the hull of this boat *Mayflower* and found it satisfactory, but that he did not issue a certificate as the owners had not a qualified Captain on her. They asked Davis to obtain for them a suitable man to fill this position if he could pick up one for them at Kingston and June 10, 1912, Davis informed the Hudsons in writing that he had not been able to obtain a Captain and that until a suitable man had been secured, passengers were not to be carried on the boat.

"On May 28th," Mr. Nickle's letter to the Honourable Mr. Hazen continued, "the owners, the Hudson brothers, had told Davis that they would not carry passengers until a proper Captain had been secured and Davis had no knowledge that passengers had been carried between May 28th and June 10th or thereafter; he thought the steamer was being run as a tugboat and to mails *(sic)* as they had a legal right to do.

"Mr. Davis has no supervision whatsoever over tugs..." concluded the letter. "If he had had such knowledge that the *Mayflower* was carrying paying customers, he would have at once notified the Department and taken steps to have compelled a cessation of passenger operation by the owners."

Commissioner Pringle was not about to let Davis off the hot seat. In his own letter to Minister Hazen, he points out that Davis could have made sure John Hudson's operation was stopped and that "the boat was tied up."

"Davis says this was not his duty; that it was the duty of the Chief Official of the customs, and no doubt he relies on the section 589 of the Act which says he doesn't have to do more than he did."

However, Pringle studied the complete Inland Waters Act and found a provision making it the duty of the inspector to notify the customs officer of all irregularities. Pringle pointed out that Davis knew Hudson was travelling without a proper master because he wrote to him advising him to stop the practice. He should have notified the customs office at the same time that he was writing Hudson.

"He could have notified the Chief Officer of Customs and the Chief Officer of Customs could have taken steps to have the boat detained," Pringle wrote. "Or he could have notified the Department and you as Minister, could have directed steps to be taken."

Both Nickle and Pringle knew that Davis' future with the government was hanging in the balance. Nickle wanted to save the man's career. And Pringle? "I thought it well that you should know my position, not that I care one iota about Mr. Davis' criticism as I feel that I could not have done less than I did in my report," wrote Pringle to Hazen.

Throughout the hearing and then subsequently on the front pages of the *Montreal Gazette* and Ottawa's *The Evening Journal*, Davis was censured for turning a blind eye to Hudson's staffing problems. It is interesting to note that at no time was the hull inspector placed under the gun for failing to spot the structural weaknesses in the *Mayflower*. The question of whether or not there was a licensed captain at her helm had little importance in the final analysis of the sinking of the stern-wheeler. The real fault lay in the design, construction and subsequent modification of the ship that had passed, aside from the matter of the captain's papers, a supposedly rigorous government inspection just months before she sank.

There is no doubt that, if Davis had blown the whistle on Jack Hudson, the *Mayflower* would have been forced to carry just cargo and mail, and the men and woman who died on her sunken deck would have lived to see 1913. It is also true that if Inspector Davis had caught the flaw in the ship's oakum, or if Engine Inspector Laurie had noticed the modifications to the stern-wheeler's paddles, the *Mayflower* could have been repaired and would have sailed on the lake in safety — with or without a licensed skipper.

Marine experts at the hearing put it down to bad engineering on the part of the Hudson brothers. A look through wreck reports in the government files would have shown those same experts that it was the design of the *Mayflower* that was at fault and the ship should never have been allowed out onto open water.

Back in 1889 the 105-foot steamer *Armstrong* was enroute from Morristown, New York to Brockville, Ontario when suddenly, without warning, the ship sank. According to passengers on the *Armstrong*, the American-registered ship sank stern-first into the waters of the St. Lawrence River. The ship took on water with little prior notice and sank almost immediately.

The *Armstrong* was longer and wider (31 feet) than the *Mayflower*, and sat deeper in the water (9.4 feet). But both ships had the same design and sank in the same fashion. And both ships had passed hull and engine inspections in the springs of the years that they sank.

Everyone on board the *Armstrong* survived the June 30 sinking, thanks to rescuers who stormed out from the Belleville harbour to assist the stranded in their lifeboats. However, the *R. Gaskin*, a wrecking schooner, sank while trying to raise the *Armstrong* and a number of crew members died.

The *Armstrong* was brought to the surface in 1890, taken to dry dock in Ogdensburg and, after being modified, was returned to active duty. The *Gaskin* was left on the bottom.

The *Armstrong* was too flat and too heavy in the stern to ply the Great Lakes. The *Mayflower* was a scaled-down version of the *Armstrong* and suffered the same problem, albeit on a scaled-down fashion on a scaled-down lake.

Even though she did not pass certification and there wasn't a master on board, most of the passengers and crew aboard the *Mayflower* would have lived, as was the case with the *Armstrong*, if the lifeboat had been attached to the stern.

The statutes covering the use of lifeboats by steamers such as the *Mayflower* were not well written back in 1912. Vessels her size were required to carry lifeboats on board.

However, there was a clause in the act that allowed ships travelling on the Ottawa River, above the city of Ottawa, to use a towable life-raft, provided the river was no more than a mile wide.

The Madawaska River qualified as a body of water covered in that special clause. But what about the section of the river/lake where it is two-to-three-miles wide? That is where the rule was ambiguous. There the rules called for the ship's lifeboat to be "on board thereof or attached thereto." Captains along the waterway interpreted 'thereto' to mean towed, and, despite objections from the marine inspectors, the ship masters got away with towing their lifeboats.

The Marine and Fisheries Department tried to get around the ambiguity of the legislation by ordering its inspectors to persuade the steamship owners that they were required to keep life-rafts on board their ships. Without a strong piece of legislation to back up that verbal request, the inspectors' wishes were ignored.

"The owners have defeated me in the argument and have gone back to towing them (lifeboats)," reported Mr. Davis. "The captains say they are more likely to use them if they are towed behind because they use them to take people on and off the steamships and the average accident is where a passenger falls overboard or where something occurs whereby the boats have to go out and get someone and this can only be done if she is towed behind."

This was the case in 1911 when the *Mayflower* sank . It was easy to tug at the stern line and pull the raft up to the side of the ship when the *Mayflower* began to take on water. Passengers had little difficulty climbing into the pointer, even as the *Mayflower* sank under them. If the life-raft had been on the roof of the ship when she sank that first time, it would have been a much slower process to free the lifeboat and, in all likelihood, passengers would have gotten wet.

In 1912 when the *Mayflower* sank again, it is doubtful that having a life-raft on board would have saved any lives. At least that was the opinion of Frank McDonnell, the assistant chairman of the Marine and Fisheries steamboat-inspection board. He testified that if the life-raft had been on the roof of the ship, strapped down and covered by a tarp, the crew wouldn't have had time to free it before the *Mayflower* settled on the bottom.

"I think that if the lifeboat had been on top, some of those good swimmers would have gone in the dark after the life-boat and no one would have been saved because they couldn't find it," testified Jack Hudson's brother, Henry, agreeing with McDonnell.

Not everyone agreed with Hudson. Commissioner Pringle questioned the practice of dragging a life-raft from the stern of the ship without a back-up raft on the roof. "I don't see myself what good that boat would have been on such occasion as this tied to the stern of the *Mayflower* when the *Mayflower* sank, except to designate where she was, because she would be sticking right up in the air."

Reviewing both sides of the life-raft argument points out the futility of the exercise. Regardless of whether the regulations called for the *Mayflower* to carry a pointer on top or drag it from the stern, the fact is that the owner of the vessel did neither.

It was a criminal act to leave the ship's most important piece of life-saving equipment tied to the Barry's Bay dock. Why did he do it?

# John Charles Hudson

The amount of data that exists today concerning the make-up of the *Mayflower* is surprising. Even the smallest detail of the ship's construction can be found in the records. For example, her top speed under steam, when there was no wind, was seven miles per hour and even the size of the water pipe leading into her boiler (1-1/4 inches) has been duly noted.

When it comes to itemizing the details of the life of her owner, however, the inventory is not so complete. John Charles Hudson died an enigma. On the one hand he was the township reeve, giving selflessly of his time to work for the good of the community and, on the other side of the coin, he was the negligent boat owner quick to lie to

**John Hudson.**

Photograph — the Jean Richter Collection

government inspectors and ready and willing to travel without a proper captain. His worst sin was leaving his lifeboat tied to the dock on the one trip he really needed it.

The unsigned note accusing Hudson of drunkenness had an effect on the way the *Mayflower* inquest was handled. Almost every witness who took the stand was asked about the condition of Hudson the day the ship went down. Like the old 'Do you still beat your wife?' routine, Hudson was damned even by the denials.

"There was nothing the matter with Hudson the day that the *Mayflower* was lost. He was the sort of character you could not tell what condition he was in. He was jovial and everyone seemed to know him. It was 'Jack here' and 'Jack there'. He was talking to everyone and seemed to know what he was doing. He walked straight."

That was the way that Henry Leach, the travelling salesman who sailed with Hudson the afternoon of November 12, remembered the shipowner. Even though Leach was very critical of Hudson and the condition of his passenger-ship operation, he stopped short of accusing him of being drunk on that last day.

"Now there is a question which I do not altogether like to ask you about, but your brother is dead and I do not think anything should be said in regard to his character if it is not true and it should be cleared up. Was your brother sober on the night of the accident so far as you know?"

Justice Pringle was blunt in the questioning of Henry Hudson.

"As far as I know. I made enquiries from the hotel keeper where he stopped when he was at Barry's Bay and he told me he was strictly sober," testified Henry. "As far as I know anything about it, he was sober."

"The man is gone," Pringle pressed on with his questioning, "and I think it should be made clear. Somebody has said that he hadn't been sober for a period of twelve months."

"That is false," Henry Edward Hudson emphatically stated.

Be that as it may, there is probably an ounce or two of truth in the statement that Jack Hudson was known to take a drink now and then. A clipping collection compiled by the volunteer staff at the Combermere Madonna House Museum keeps alive the stories of the people who remembered the *Mayflower* days. There is mention of the *Mayflower* moonlight cruises and the card games and drinks that were enjoyed on board the stern-wheeler. A picture in the early 1970s shows a scuba diver retrieving artifacts from the wreck of the ship. One of the items brought from the bottom was an unopened liquor bottle.

The *Mayflower* sank because of foul weather and the weakening of the oakum in her hull. Whether or not Hudson was sober had little bearing on the demise of his ship. However, lives were at stake and the conduct of the owner prior to November 12, 1912, was in contradiction to community standards and the law. Perhaps if Hudson had been a sober, God-fearing, law-abiding man, his ship would have been in accordance with the law and no one would have died that night.

Hudson went down with his ship, so it was never learned why he left his lumberman's pointer tied to the dock. Several years after his death it was revealed that at dockside, prior to the departure of the *Mayflower* on that fatal trip home, Hudson was warned not to go out on the lake — weather conditions were beginning to turn sour. Hudson ignored the warning, and did not reattach the lifeboat. The night was cold and dark — a drink or two would have helped warm the innards of Captain Jack. Had alcohol clouded his reasoning powers?

Probably not. Hudson was taking a body back to Palmer Rapids as a favour to his friends. With a stiff, cold wind blowing, Hudson probably left the life-raft behind to reduce the drag on the *Mayflower* and speed her arrival at Combermere and Palmer Rapids.

Jack Hudson was a man with too many irons in the fire. He was involved in so many vital activities that his own family had trouble keeping track of him. His wife, Margaret, was not alarmed when her husband didn't show up at their Combermere home. She thought he had stayed the night in Palmer Rapids, a thing he would normally do when nightfall caught up with him. The night before the sinking, Hudson had stayed in Barry's Bay.

A man with too many interests runs the danger of not doing any one task well. Hudson's attendance at county council was spotty. In addition to the hotel, the *Mayflower* and local government, Jack and his wife owned a two-hundred-acre farm near Canoe Lake. He often listed his occupation as 'farmer'.

He also owned, together with his brother Henry, a sawmill near the river. It was apparently successful, which could be attributed to the skills of Henry, who was an engineer.

Jack was a maverick, a man willing to operate outside of the rules. He had no qualms about lying to the hull and engine inspectors or submitting to them the name of a captain who had left his employ a year earlier. He ignored the rules to his own benefit. And, through loyalty to his friends, he was ready to turn his back on safety and spit into the eye of a winter storm.

The modifications that Jack Hudson made to his vessel were typical of his personality. He must have put little thought into the structural strains caused by the removal of some of the water-wheel blades and the readjustment of the remaining slats. When the *Armstrong* sank without warning, her sinking, like the *Mayflower's*, was a big news item. Hudson must have been aware of the layout problems of the *Armstrong* and her similarities to his own ship. Despite this he went ahead and customized the *Mayflower*.

As early as May 1912 Hudson knew that the design of his *Mayflower* was shoddy. The boat was flat and with the blades of the wheel slapping the water the ship, as mentioned previously, was very hard to manage in a strong wind. An episode with the Anglican Archbishop illustrates the problems Hudson had with the construction of his 'Jewel of Lake Kamaniskeg.'

The steamships on Lake Kamaniskeg were launched for the start of the season at the end of the second week of May. Shortly after getting his boat into the water, Hudson played host to an important visitor. A high-ranking Anglican minister, Archbishop Hamilton, took a ride on the ship one very blustery day in May. The Archbishop's voyage was rough and his faith in the seaworthiness of the *Mayflower* was very low.

"Only last May he (the Archbishop) had an experience on her. He got aboard her at Barry's Bay to go to Combermere. A stiff wind was blowing at the time and the passengers had to lend a hand to help her leave the wharf. When she got out a little way in the water she almost turned over.

"The Lord must have been with Hudson and the Archbishop that blowing May day. The ship righted herself. A short time later more steam was got up and she was able to make the journey down the river without accident or further adventure," read a report in the local paper.

Despite the misadventure, Archbishop Hamilton, the Anglican authority for the Upper Ottawa Valley, was to have travelled on the *Mayflower* again. The Archbishop had planned to sail on November 12, 1912. He had phoned ahead to book passage on the ship as he was making a scheduled visit to see Reverend S. D. Hague, the Combermere Anglican vicar. If Reverend Hague had not decided to surprise the Archbishop by meeting him with his horse and buggy at the GTR station in Barry's Bay, Archbishop Hamilton would have been on the stern-wheeler the night she sank.

His Grace stayed at the Hudson Hotel the night the vessel was lost and he learned first-hand from Hudson's mother that the *Mayflower* was missing. Upon his return to Barry's Bay, he thanked God for sparing his life.

Now Hudson might not have been quick to fix the faults of his ship, but, when she started sinking, he did everything to save her and the lives of the passengers. When the water started rushing in, Hudson didn't try to save himself.

His first thought was to save the ship. He yelled at Parcher to sound the ship's horn and he then rushed back towards the sinking stern in an effort to shut down the boiler. He didn't want an explosion to destroy the ship and kill the passengers who were scrambling onto her sinking deck.

He was brave, he was a maverick, a law-breaker, a law-maker, happy-go-lucky and yes, Jack Hudson was a family man.

The Hudson family had been in the Combermere district for more than sixty years. Elizabeth and John moved from the city of Ottawa to Radcliffe Township when the lumber trade first began. Their arrival in the 1850s guaranteed them a valuable tract of free land.

The Hudsons had two sons and a daughter. The daughter married a Waddington and built a home next to the family farm. Likewise Henry built a place near his parents' home. He apparently owned a home and property in Barry's Bay.

John Hudson was married to Margaret Mahon Hudson, a woman eleven years his junior. It was a mixed marriage, John was an Anglican and Margaret remained a Roman Catholic. The couple had only one son, Edward, who was born in Combermere.

The family holdings were alongside the Opeongo Road. All told, the Hudson family had six hundred acres of prime

**The *Mayflower* sailed the waters of Lake Kamaniskeg in the pioneer days of Renfrew County. Life was tough, as the above photo indicates. Pictured is an Opeongo Trail settler's house taken in 1901. The Hudson family lived on the Opeongo Trail.**

Photograph — The Charles MacNamara Collection 227155056

land on both sides of the Line, east of the Madawaska River and west of Lake Diamond. The original Hudson farm land abutted the property of John Waddington, Jack's brother-in-law. They owned a lumber-yard and most likely had timber rights in the Lake Kamaniskeg district.

The Hudson hotel was at the bank of the Madawaska River on a road that is now Highway 62. Until the fire of 1911 Hudson kept his lake ships beached near the hotel. They were destroyed in the fire.

Jack took an interest in politics early in life. In 1906 he helped with the formation of Radcliffe Township. (Prior to 1906 Radcliffe was part of Raglan Township). Until his death he was the township's first and only reeve. He represented Radcliffe on county council in the town of Pembroke.

As the first family of Radcliffe Township, Jack and his wife were constantly taking part in community and family outings.

Jack's social and political accomplishments were regularly reported in the papers of Pembroke, Eganville and Renfrew. Consider the following item that appeared in two papers of his day:

*RENFREW MERCURY, JULY 31, 1908.— St. Pauls Church, Combermere was the scene of a pretty wedding on Wednesday the 15th, when Miss Gertrude Waddington was married to Mr. Fraser Reid, the popular official of the corundum mine at Cobalt. The bride who was attired in white silk with chiffon trimming was attended by her cousin, Miss Annie Dennison, while Mr. J. Waddington assisted the groom. The bride was given away by the popular owner of the steamer 'Mayflower' her uncle Mr. J. Hudson.*

*The marriage service was performed by Reverend Mr. Archer of Winchester assisted by Reverand M. J.*

*O'Donnell, the present incumbent of the parish. Mr. Roy Dennison resided at the organ with music appropriate to the occasion. After the wedding ceremony the bridal party and their friends to the number of about fifty partook of breakfast under the hospitable roof of Mrs. Hudson, the grandmother of the bride. After which the happy couple took the boat the **Mayflower** to Barry's Bay on their way to Metagami where they will spend a few days before proceeding to their new home in Cobalt. A large number of their friends accompanied them to Barry's Bay and gave them a huge send-off.*

John Charles Hudson is buried in a cemetery within sight of his mother's hotel (now the Hudson House). His stone reads: "Thy Trials Ended, Thy Rest Is Won."

Photograph — S. Weir

The social pages of the *Eganville Leader* made mention in the December 8 issue of Mrs. J. Hudson, concerning her visit to Barry's Bay.

*Mrs. John Hudson of Combermere is guesting with Miss Annie Sinclair of Barry's Bay.*

In the Pembroke papers there is mention of how Mrs. J. Hudson visited the Craigmont picnic in 1911 with her sisters. She visited again in 1912. The couple seemed to be a fun-loving, outgoing, civic-minded pair.

Jack and his wife represented the pioneer spirit of the Ottawa Valley. There was no business he wouldn't have a go at; there was nothing he wouldn't give to his community and his friends.

When Hudson's body was recovered from the sunken *Mayflower* it was taken to a cemetery across the road from his mother's hotel. There, near the grave of his pilot, Aaron Parcher, the ship's owner was laid to rest.

His epitaph carved into the headstone is appropriate. **"Thy Trials Ended, Thy Rest Is Won."**

# CHAPTER SEVEN

## A Tale Of Two Bodies

It took three long weeks, a cross-Canada train ride, a shipwreck and the death of nine people before the body of John Brown could finally be laid to rest. It took six months of fruitless searching above and below the surface of Lake Kamaniskeg before the corpse of George Bothwell was recovered and buried. The history of the *Mayflower* is the story of a shipwreck, but it is also the tale of two dead men who didn't want to be put into their graves.

Brown's was the body in the coffin, that macabre wooden box that saved the lives of three Ottawa salesmen. If he had not died a mysterious death in Yorkton, Saskatchewan, the trio wouldn't have had a pine box to use as a life-raft. They would never have reached that small island alive.

Bothwell, on the other hand, was a strong swimmer and should have been able to make it to land under his own steam. Dubbed the man most likely to survive, he was last seen diving into Lake Kamaniskeg just as the steamship shuddered and sank. It wasn't until the spring of 1913 that his bloated corpse was recovered.

The news of the rescue of Bothwell's travelling companions from the frozen shore of Gull Island set the country abuzz. Their use of Brown's coffin had overtones of Herman Melleville's *Moby Dick,* a classic even in those days. People wanted to know the biography of the man inside the box. How did he die? The answer to that question was as strange as the sinking of the *Mayflower*.

John Brown was raised in Palmer Rapids, a small town that huddles against the Madawaska River, south of the village of Combermere. He was the oldest son in a very large family. He had six sisters and five brothers.

In 1911, a year before the sinking, Brown left his home in the Upper Ottawa Valley and went out west. He was on his way to help his sister and her husband, Robert Pachal, with their dairy operation outside the Saskatchewan city of Yorkton; he was twenty-seven years of age.

Brown arrived in Yorkton and immediately started to help with the Pachal herd. Their farm was close to a growing city, and the Pachals and Brown were optimistic about its chances for success. Like most people starting out on their own in a new area, Brown found he needed an outside job to supplement his farming income.

**This is the farm where John Brown was born and raised. It was located in Raglan Township near Schutt. This photograph was taken in 1931, nineteen years after Brown's death.**

Photograph — The Schutt Collection

He took part-time employment with a manufacturing firm. After the herd had been milked each morning, Brown would report to the railroad station and, with the assistance of a helper, pick up freight, load it onto a horse-drawn rig and transport it back to the manufacturing plant.

The route Brown travelled from the station to the factory wound its way through a stretch of uninhabited prairie grassland. It was Brown's habit to carry a loaded long gun. He would bag game on his way to and from the railroad yard. The gun was the cause of his death and the catalyst for the *Mayflower* disaster.

"This particular morning, November 7th, 1912, while returning from the station, he was accompanied by a young man who drove the team while he (Brown) crossed a slough, apparently for the purpose of shooting some prairie chickens. The man in the wagon saw Brown walk through the long grass and bushes until shortly (thereafter) before the report of a rifle (sic) and thinking Brown had shot a bird he drove on," read the *Eganville Leader*.

The assistant took the cargo to the factory loading dock. He tied up the team and sat back to wait for John Brown to come walking down the lane carrying his freshly shot bird. He waited, but Brown did not show his face. Eventually realizing that Brown was in trouble, he alerted the factory manager and a search-party was sent out to look for the missing man. They returned to the bush where John Brown had last been seen.

It didn't take long for the men to find Brown. He was sitting in the grass, a stone's throw from the road. His rifle was in his lap, there was blood all over his face. He hadn't bagged a bird, he had shot himself.

"They found him in a half-sitting position with a .32 rifle ball (bullet) lodged in his brain. The charge entered a little above the left eye. Brown was at once taken to the hospital but surgical aid was unavailable. He died about 3:00 p.m. of the same day," reported the newspapers of the day.

The cause of the shooting was never officially determined. Brown either tripped and shot himself or he committed suicide. The rumour mill of the day pegged it suicide.[8] Nevertheless he was permitted a church burial back in Ontario. His families, the Browns and the Boehmes, made arrangements to have him interred in the graveyard of the Evangelical Church in Schutt, a village west of Palmer Rapids.

Brown's body was sent east on November 10, 1912, three days after his death. Robert Pachal, his brother-in-law, agreed to accompany the remains back to Palmer Rapids.

It was two days later that the coffin and Pachal arrived in Barry's Bay aboard the Grand Trunk Railroad. The steam-engine train pulled into the village station after the *Mayflower* had sailed for Combermere.

The telephone, invented in 1876, was, in 1912, still not universally owned. There were many households in Renfrew County without one. Pachal, upon arriving at the station in Barry's Bay, couldn't phone his father-in-law, Herman Brown, in Palmer Rapids. Instead he had to contact a relative of Herman's in Combermere. He called

[8] *The Ottawa Valley newspapers in 1912 were not always reliable. The Eganville paper had Brown a married man with a daughter. He, according to his family who still live in the area, died a bachelor. The papers were probably referring to his sister and brother-in-law with whom he went to live. The rumours could have been caused by shoddy reportage in the local papers.*

William Boehme, a member of Hudson's township council, and told him that he had John Brown's body and that he and a number of train passengers were in Barry's Bay waiting for the return of the *Mayflower*.

By this time John Hudson was planning to scrub the return trip to Barry's Bay. Hudson knew that he would not be able to make it to Barry's Bay and back before nightfall. He was also very concerned about the approaching winter storm. Boehme was able to convince

**Above left, William and Louisa Boehme.**
**Above right, the neglected grave of William Murphy is in an overgrown Rockingham cemetery. The *Mayflower* victim is buried beside his sister.**

Photograph — Jean Richter Collection     Photograph — S. Weir

Hudson that he should help get Brown's body home as soon as possible, and, when a travelling salesman bought a ticket to travel from Combermere to Barry's Bay, it suddenly made economic sense to take the risk. Boehme and a friend of his, William Murphy, climbed aboard; they wanted to meet Pachal and his silent charge.

If Robert Pachal hadn't contacted William Boehme, it is possible that Hudson would have delayed the return trip until the morrow. The *Mayflower* would have lived to sail

another day. All the ifs in the world, however, aren't worth the value of even one life-jacket; Pachal, Boehme, Murphy and Hudson had a date with destiny that night. All four drowned in the freezing waters of Lake Kamaniskeg.

John Brown's body might have been the cause of the disaster. But it was also a life-saver. When the steamship *Ruby* rescued the men, they wouldn't leave the island without taking along the coffin — they owed Brown that much.

**Robert Pachal and his brother-in-law, John Brown, are buried toe-to-toe in a Schutt graveyard. Brown is buried with his father Herman and mother Augusta. Pachal is buried alone.**

Photograph — S. Weir

When the grieving family came for the coffin they found out that they had to make funeral arrangements for four; Murphy, Brown, Boehme and Pachal. The Brown family either couldn't afford or didn't want to return Pachal's coffin to his family in Yorkton, instead he was buried toe-to-toe with his brother-in-law John Brown.

Brown and Pachal's funeral and burial were held in Shutt. There on a hill overlooking the Raglan Heights and Boehme's Mountain one can find the graves of Brown, his parents and Robert Pachal.[9]

The whispered talk of Brown's possible suicide ended long before the body of the *Mayflower's* last victim was found. It took six months of searching before the remains of George Bothwell were discovered.

At twenty-seven years of age, Bothwell was in his prime. A clean-shaven, broad-shouldered man, Bothwell was considered one of Ottawa's leading bachelors. A strong swimmer and all-around athlete, Bothwell was often admired for, as the society columnist wrote in his day, his "splendid physique." He was an active member of the Masonic Lodge.

Bothwell had come to Canada in 1906 from his family home in Aberdeen, Scotland. A year after arriving in the capital city, he took employment with the F. J. Castle Company. Although only a travelling salesman with the produce company he was considered a member of the company's executive and had a bright future.

The *Mayflower* journey was part of his regular circuit through the area. He had left Ottawa the day before the sinking.

[9] *Pachal's wife and daughter moved back to Renfrew County following the funeral. His daughter still lives in Schutt.*

When the *Mayflower* was straining to make headway against the strong cold winds of November, Bothwell, a seasoned Ontario traveller, decided to stay warm and dry in the main hold. He pulled up a seat beside an overturned barrel and played cards with his salesmen companions. Survivors reported seeing him dive through an open doorway into the lake just as the *Mayflower* shuddered and sank.

Back in Ottawa, anxious comrades awaited news of the missing man. When it was reported that three Ottawa survivors had been found, it was assumed that George was one of them. *The Evening Journal* expressed it this way: "Friends of Mr. Bothwell who knew his powers expected his name to come in amongst the list of the saved."

It wasn't. Divers crawled through the wreck and surrounding lake bed looking for the bodies. All of the dead were accounted for, except Bothwell. The lake was dragged and search-parties continued to patrol the shore line looking for the dead man. The search was called off when the lake froze over.

On April 24, 1913, Bothwell was found by a local man, John Lavelle. "The remains were discovered on the rocks on the east shore of the river nearly opposite to where the wreck occurred."

According to the story that appeared in the *Pembroke Observer*, the grisly find took place where another body had been found six months before. "It will be remembered that it was about this spot that Captain Parcher's body was recovered on the river after the tragic affair."

*This Week In The Madawaska Valley*, a Barry's Bay newspaper, recounted a very interesting myth that has sprung up about the finding of Bothwell's body. Back in November 1912 a native Canadian, helping in the search for Bothwell, supposedly saw a man on shore waving a white hanky.

When a search of the shore was conducted no trace of the man with the handkerchief could be found. In the spring of the next year, the man returned to the spot where he had seen the waving hanky. That is where Bothwell's body was located.

George Bothwell's body was transported back to Ottawa immediately after it was examined by the authorities. Shortly thereafter the last vicitim of the *Mayflower* was buried.

# CHAPTER EIGHT

It was February 3, 1913, when Justice Pringle issued his seven-page investigation into the wreck of the *Mayflower*. The document was given to the federal cabinet, along with more than one hundred pages of inquest testimonies, photographs, letters and government documents.

The report laid the blame squarely on Hudson and the modifications that were made to the *Mayflower*. It criticized the government for the way boats of the day were inspected, noting that even though vessels were regularly inspected there was no mechanism in place to enforce the shipping laws of the land.

Based on the report's findings, the government made several changes to the shipping laws, most notably the section dealing with life-rafts. As well, the way in which the inland marine fleet was inspected was overhauled.

Because Pringle cited government mishandling as far as the ship's inspection was concerned, an effort was made on the part of relatives of the victims to get redress from the federal government.

After the *Mayflower* sank it was MP Gerald White (Renfrew North) from Pembroke who pushed the federal government into action. He was instrumental in getting a rescue team on the wreck site almost immediately.

When it came time to help the relatives seek compensation from the government, however, it was not White who took up their cause. White was a Conservative back-bencher, a member of the party which, under Bordon, was in power. It wouldn't do for White to attack his own.

No, the flag was carried by the Honourable George Graham, the Liberal member for Renfrew South. As the former Minister of Canals and Inland Waterways during the Laurier years, Graham was well qualified to dog the Marine and Fisheries minister.

Graham was born in Eganville in 1859 and educated in Morrisburg, Ontario. A journalist by trade, at one time he was the managing director of the *Brockville Recorder*. He also worked for the *Morrisburg Herald* and was, briefly, an associate editor of the *Ottawa Free Press*. A Methodist by birth, Graham was often touted as a successor to Sir Wilfred Laurier.

**George Perry Graham, MPP for Renfrew South, fought long and hard for compensation for the families of the *Mayflower* victims.**

Photograph — Ontario Archives L 977

Originally active in provincial politics, Graham was leader of the Liberal opposition in the 1907 Ontario legislature. He sat in the federal House for Brockville in the same year and served until his defeat in 1911 (while he was minister of Canals and Inland Waterways). In February of 1912 he won a seat for the Liberals in a Renfrew South by-election.

Speaking in the House, Graham went after Hazen, the minister in charge of the investigation of 1912/1913. The year was 1916.

"About a year ago (actually it was four years) a sad accident occurred in the County of Renfrew between Combermere and Barry's Bay, by which several persons lost their lives. Mr. Pringle who conducted the investigation made a very strong report as to the unseaworthiness of the vessel, the *Mayflower*, which would imply faulty inspection," spoke Graham in the House.

The Minister of Marine and Fisheries, the Honourable Hazen, replied: "Not faulty inspection. I understand that the boat should not have been allowed by the Collector of Customs to leave port."

"I thought at the time that the boat had been proved to be unseaworthy, even if equipped with all the appliances mentioned," pressed Mr. Graham. "She went down through somebody's fault with the sad loss of life. I thought that under the circumstances the Government might have seen its way clear... to give some aid, the wreck having been at least partly due to the neglect of some Government official. Is there any such provision in these estimates?"

Mr. Hazen did not agree. "My recollection is that the *Mayflower* was wrecked some three years ago in the Madawaska River: that she left during a heavy storm although the captain had been warned of the danger; and, she did not have proper lifeboats or apparatus, there was loss of life. I do not remember that there was a suggestion of any liability, legal or moral attaching to the Government in connection with it. It would not be a matter particularly for my department."

"I think I made the suggestion myself," said Mr. Graham, "and the Minister of Finance said that the Government might consider it. I do not attempt to make out a case of legal liability on the Government: but I thought that, as some person in the employ of the Government was at fault, the Department of Marine and Fisheries might well recommend a small grant to those who were left behind."

At this point in the February 11, 1916 debate, the Minister of Finance, the Honourable Mr. Murphy broke in, "My recollection coincides with that of the honourable member for Renfrew. The inquiry established the fact that the boat should not have been given a licence as it was in a dilapidated and dangerous condition. The warning referred to by the minister was given to the captain on the night of the storm. The boat practically foundered."

In 1917 Graham gave up his Renfrew South seat and successfully contested the Essex South riding. Even though he had switched seats, he refused to give up his fight for the victims of the *Mayflower*.

Mr. Graham brought the matter up in the House on three different occasions over a four-year period with no apparent success. And on another front, a law firm was looking for compensation for one of its clients. In the files of the Canadian Archives in Ottawa there is a letter from John Hunter, a Toronto barrister, requesting a copy of the Pringle report with a view to determining the question of liability. No mention in the letter is made as to the identity of Hunter's client.

A search of all government files and contact with some of the relatives of the victims of the sinking has failed to uncover any compensation payments. The government's position was that Hudson was at fault and not the Ministry of Marine and Fisheries. The minister's own papers, on file at the University of New Brunswick, do not mention the *Mayflower* — many Hazen documents were destroyed when the Parliament Buildings burned.

The government took the position that Hudson was at fault and not the Ministry of Marine and Fisheries.

So, what exactly did the report say? What follows are excerpts from the eight-page report that was written by Pringle and addressed to the Honourable J. D. Hazen.

"Immediately on receiving notice of my appointment I deemed it expedient and advisable to proceed to Barry's Bay and the scene of the wreck, as I learned the divers were engaged near the wreck in a search for the body of George Bothwell, and I considered it important that I should avail myself of their services before they finished their work. Consequently I proceeded to Barry's Bay on the morning of 21st November 1912, arriving there that afternoon, and finding it impossible to reach the wreck that day, I spent several hours in interviewing the parties who were likely to throw some light on the cause of the accident.

"On the morning of the 22nd November 1912 I proceeded on the Steamer *Ruby* to the scene of the wreck with the divers and others who were assisting in the search for George Bothwell's body. Having heard rumours as to the unsoundness of the Steamer *Mayflower*, I directed the divers to make borings from stem to stern of the hull and also to cut out with a chisel pieces of timber in the hull towards the stern of the boat, in order to ascertain if the timbers were sound. This the divers did, and they found the timbers to be perfectly sound as appears in the evidence of Benoit Rouleau and

James Scott attached hereto. I also had them make a thorough examination as to the cause of the leak, as it was quite evident from what I learned that the Steamer *Mayflower* had not come in contact or collision with anything that would have caused her to leak.

"The divers examined the seams, particularly towards the stern of the boat they found that the seams were quite open, the oakum loose and in places Benoit Rouleau had no difficulty in running the piece of glass through the planking.

"I have arrived at the following conclusions: The Steamer *Mayflower* was built in 1903, and placed in commission in 1904. She was a boat of very light draught, owing to the fact that she was built for the purpose of operating on a route where, in places, there was very shallow water. She was 77 ft. in length, 18 ft. in width and 4 ft. in depth and was known as a 'Stern-Wheeler.' She plied between Barry's Bay and Havergal calling at Combermere. Her engines were placed one on each side of that portion of the deck that formed the sides of the opening in which the paddle-wheel revolved and from the evidence of Henry E. Hudson, M. R. Davis and others, I am of the opinion that certain changes having been made to the paddles the effect was to place a greater strain on the boat, and there being a fairly heavy wind on the night of the 12th November 1912 the strain increased and the seams were opened in that portion of the hull near the paddle-wheel where the water rushed in very rapidly, as before anyone on board noticed the water the stern was practically submerged."

"It was a sudden filling up otherwise the fireman would have noticed the water as it would have affected the fire. According to the evidence, the water was not noticed until it was rushing in over the deck at both sides of the boat where there were openings, I should say about the middle of the boat.

"After proceeding about seven or eight miles from Barry's Bay and having reached a short distance into what is known as Lake Kamaniskeg, an expansion of the Madawaska River, about nine o'clock of the night of the 12th of November 1912 she suddenly sprang a leak, and sank almost immediately after it was noticed.

"As I heard many rumours regarding John Hudson, I think it is only fair to say that from the evidence it would appear that John Hudson was a man who had been for many years engaged in boating on the Madawaska River and that on the night in question, he was perfectly competent to take charge of the Steamer *Mayflower* and that both Delaney and Parcher were also competent men.

"I find that the *Mayflower* was running from early in the season of 1912 until the night she sank, absolutely contrary to the law, Hudson not having obtained the certificate required by the Shipping Act and she was running without a qualified Master.

"I find that on the night of the 12th November 1912, the night the *Mayflower* sank, that no lifeboat was attached as required by law, the evidence being that the lifeboat had broken loose the evening before and instead of it being reattached to the *Mayflower*, had been left tied to the wharf at Barry's Bay and in this respect Hudson was guilty of gross negligence.

"Why was the *Mayflower* permitted to run and carry passengers from early in the season of 1912 until the night she sank without authority? It was a matter of common knowledge throughout the country that she was running and carrying passengers. This question presents difficulties to my mind. The Inspector of Hulls, M. R. Davis in his evidence is asked, Q. There was no certificate issued for 1912? A. No sir. Q.Then as a matter of fact he was contravening the law in operating his boat at all? A. Yes sir, and I warned him about that. Q. And in carrying passengers? A. Yes, and I warned him of that and he promised me he would stop carrying passengers. It also appears that M. R. Davis Esq. wrote Hudson Bros. of Combermere on the 10th of June 1912 advising Hudson Bros. to drop the passenger business and telling them they had no right to carry passengers until they had a proper captain, and that he was unable to issue the certificate.

"I am irresistibly drawn to the conclusion that when Hudson promised M. R. Davis that he would stop carrying passengers as M. R. Davis says he did, that he, M. R. Davis, must have known and did know that Hudson was acting illegally, and I consider that it would have been at least wisdom on the part of M. R. Davis, when he saw that no proper steps were being taken to stop the running of the *Mayflower*, to have notified the Department of Marine and Fisheries so that the Minister could have directed some person or persons to take the neccesary steps to seize and detain the boat.

"I find after investigation and examination of officials that there does not appear to be any official in the Department of Marine and Fisheries specially charged with the duty of seeing that vessels which have failed to obtain a certificate as required by the act, are prevented from carrying passengers.

"I find in examining the steamboat inspection reports for the past few years that there are approximately 2,100 vessels inspected in each year, and that out of this number, a very few fail to obtain certificates, and I am of the opinion that there would be no great difficulty in preventing these vessels from running and carrying passengers.

"In conclusion, permit me to recommend that an official of your Department be instructed, or if necessary, appointed, charged with the duty of seeing that no vessel be permitted to carry passengers without having first fully complied with the law, and I would further recommend that such official be empowered to take such steps as he may deem necessary in order that the many provisions of the 'Shipping Act' which are for the protection of the travelling public, are fully complied with and that in the event of non-compliance, the penalties provided by the Act be enforced."

Pringle worked hard in producing the report. He travelled to Barry's Bay and spent two days on the *Ruby* in near-winter conditions. He conducted a number of interviews throughout the Christmas period of 1912, including a session on Boxing Day. In all he heard sworn testimony from seventeen people.

In billing the government he estimated that he spent eight-and-a-half days investigating the loss of the ship. And, he spent another two-and-a-half days listening to testimony. His bill to the government? A mere $552.40, of which $212.40 went to cover costs he incurred.

**The sinking of the *Mayflower* was front-page news across the province. Ottawa's *The Evening Journal* cleared most of the front page to cover the tragedy. The reports, many of them based on second and third-hand sources, were inaccurate, but made for great reading!**

# CHAPTER NINE

The loss of the *Mayflower* was stop-the-press news across the nation... for less than four days. Before all of the bodies had been found, the *Mayflower* had sunk to the back pages, only to resurface when the ship's inquest was held and then later when relatives of the victims unsuccessfully petitioned for federal government compensation.

Tragedy became forgotten copy rather quickly in the journals of that day. Callous to forget such deep losses so quickly? There really wasn't a choice: "Times," as the saying goes, "were tough." Disasters, such as the sinking of the *Mayflower*, were regular news items. From the high seas to the waters of the Great Lakes, vessels were regularly lost; and November was always a good month for bad shipping news.

Consider the records of November and December 1912. On the first of the month the steamer barge *Juneau* took another barge, the *Lock*, in tow at Port Anne, Ontario. The tandem stopped in Belleville to pick up a load of stone destined for Toronto.

Shortly after leaving Belleville harbour, the *Juneau* sprang a leak. The *Lock* was cut loose and the steamer raced to shore. The crew manned the pumps and prayed they'd hit land before they sank beneath the surface of Lake Ontario.

Luck was with the *Juneau*. She sank right at the Cobourg town pier. The crew jumped off her deck and onto the shore just as she began her descent to the bottom of the lake.

Meanwhile the four-member crew of the *Lock* found themselves in a dangerous position. They were aboard an engineless vessel and since being cut loose from the *Juneau* had drifted along at the mercy of currents and the roaring November winds. The wind and the waves drove the stone-laden orphan onto the rocks of the Gull Lighthouse on the shores of Lake Ontario.

The crew consisted of three men and a woman. Soaking wet and near death because of the freezing fall temperatures, the four spent the night huddled near the twisted wreckage of the *Lock*, much in the way the survivors of the *Mayflower* spent their night of hell. All four crew members of the *Lock* lived through the ordeal and were able to tell their story of survival to the local press.

Six days later, the story of the crew of the *Lock* suddenly became old hat. A new sinking had scribes working overtime at news desks across the country. The CNR steamer, the *Royal George*, was wrecked off the Isle of Orleans. None of the passengers were hurt when the ship grounded on the shoals of the St. Lawrence River. However, it took nearly a week to refloat the *Royal George* from the wreck site below Quebec City.

A week after the *Royal George* went down, the *Mayflower* followed suit. And so it went on, week after week after week. Two weeks after the *Mayflower* sank, searchers were out looking for traces of the British schooner the *Merrman*. The three-masted ocean-goer went missing near Maine late in November.

At the same time a ship drama of another sort was taking place at the eastern end of Lake Superior. The *Turret*

*Crown* was adrift near Sault Ste. Marie and authorities were determined not to let her land in Canada. The vessel, bound for Georgian Bay, was discovered to be carrying passengers who were infected with smallpox. The police had their orders: the lake ship must stay away from land until the disease had run its course.

On December fourth, the late season ended the same way it had started in November. The three-masted schooner, the *Rouse Simmons*, was officially listed as lost after going missing during a Lake Michigan squall.

The body count for the *Mayflower*, the *Rouse Simmons* and the *Merrman* was under one hundred, small in number compared to the losses recorded at the start of that shipping year.

It was the era of the super ocean liner, and it was in 1912, that the pride of the Atlantic and the British White Star Line was launched into infamy. The *Titanic* sank April 14, 1912 on her maiden voyage. Close to two thousand lives were lost. The passenger liner went down after striking an iceberg in the North Atlantic close to Newfoundland.

The world was running madly into the twentieth century. The newspaper, the only source of world news, had more than just sinking ships to report. The year 1912 was very busy.

It was the year that China became a republic, ending thousands of years of monarchic rule. The Balkan League fought a war with Turkey. Suffragettes were throwing stones at Lloyd George. Winston Churchill was a new face in Parliament and madman John Schrand tried to kill former U.S. president Teddy Roosevelt.

In Canada, Sir Wilfred Laurier turned seventy-one in November and was still combative as the Leader of the Liberal Opposition in the House. Across the floor, Robert

Borden, Prime Minister and leader of the Conservative Party, was actively considering the formation of Canada's first navy.

The railroad was opening Canada's heartland to lumber companies and settlers alike. But there was still a place for the schooner, the stern-wheeler and the steamship in the commerce of the nation. Many Ontario industrialists thought water and steam were the two best ways to make the Dominion great.

In the days of the *Mayflower* one team of businessmen and local politicians had plans to build a canal from Lake Ontario to Georgian Bay so that the steamship trade could have access to Lakes Huron and Superior.

And still another group had even more grandiose ideas in the works. The Waterways Union of Canada issued a pamphlet in 1897 (just about the time Jack Hudson was building his first *Mayflower*) calling for the digging of a canal from "Lake Superior to the foothills of the Rockies."

The society wanted to dig a fifteen-foot-deep canal that would snake from lake to lake across the prairies so that the British, who were supposed to pay for this gigantic trench, could rule supreme in North America. "Everywhere the British flag will fly, our armed cruisers and ironclads will assist our Northwest Mounted Police (the forerunner of the RCMP) in patrolling the 49th parallel."

At that point in time, rail rates were still much more dear than the steamboat charges. Boat boosters claimed, and with good reason, that it was not only cheaper to ship by boat, it was often much quicker than if one used the unreliable rail lines.

Jack Hudson took this philosophy to heart when he built his first steamship in 1899. Called the *Hudson*, it was probably the first stern-wheeler to ply the waters of Lake Kamaniskeg.

The Hudson boats were built to carry corundum from the Combermere-area mines to Barry's Bay. Hudson lost his contracts in 1904 when the mine-owned steamboat, the *Ruby*, was launched on the waters of Lake Kamaniskeg.

An aerial view of Lake Kamaniskeg showing the position of Parcher (top) and Mayflower Islands. The right-hand fork of the lake leads through the Narrows to Barry's Bay. The left-hand fork is where the Madawaska River (flowing from Algonquin Park through Bark Lake) joins Lake Kamaniskeg. The lower-right fork is where the river leaves the lake for Combermere, Palmer Rapids and beyond. The Madawaska River eventually drains into the Ottawa River at Arnprior. The photograph was taken by the Ministry of Transport in 1976.

Competition among boat owners wasn't confined to the waters of Barry's Bay. The Ottawa Valley had a healthy marine industry and the shipowners managed to make a profitable living, despite the arrival of the Iron Horse and the private automobile.

Back in 1925, a Mr. H. R. Morgan gave a paper to the Ontario Historical Society in Welland Ontario. His topic? Steam navigation on the Ottawa River.

According to that early Ontario historian, the Ottawa Valley has a rich maritime tradition. In fact, in 1847 the Ottawa Forwarding Company alone had fourteen steamers operating in the waters above the city of Ottawa. Many of those ships travelled to Pembroke with a railroad transfer to carry passengers around a number of rapids.

Other transport companies used stage-coaches and paddlewheelers to move people and freight from Ottawa to Pembroke. "Flat-bottom boats and later steamboats were used on Muskrat Lake (Cobden is on the lake), Mud Lake and the Muskrat River to Pembroke landing," wrote H.R. Morgan. One steamer on the Muskrat was called the *Jason Gould*.

With so many ships plying the waters of the Upper Ottawa Valley, government inspectors had trouble reaching the many berths to examine and license the ships each season. Many captains were able to operate without interference or regulation on the part of the Federal Ministry of Marine and Fisheries. The *Mayflower* was just one of a legion of disasters that forced the government to tighten the reins on the fleet owners of the day.

Even the news of marine reform was buried by the newspaper writers of 1913. They were happy to leave their wreck stories behind and focus on another coming storm — the First World War.

# CHAPTER TEN

More people have swum above the broken bones of the *Mayflower* than ever stood upon her deck. Poor old Jack Hudson: if he could have received a dollar from every diver who would one day visit his sunken ghost ship, he could

**The broken paddle-wheel of the *Mayflower* has become a haven for schools of small fish.**

Photograph — S. Weir

easily have afforded a licensed captain and kept a better maintained vessel.

The ice comes out of Kamaniskeg Lake in late April every year. By the end of spring, sport divers are on the lake looking for the remains of the stern-wheeler. The dive season encompasses each and every weekend from June until mid-October and aquanauts have been viewing the *Mayflower* in ever increasing numbers since the 1960s when sport diving first became popular.

The water clarity is excellent. Sitting on the bottom of Kamaniskeg, a diver, at a depth of twenty-five feet, can see the shadowy bottom of his boat on the surface. And up above, if there is no chop on the water and the sun is shining in the sky, a spotter sitting in the bow of a slow-moving boat can sometimes see the submerged bones of the *Mayflower*.

If the ice hasn't taken its toll, there is a bobbing marker attached to an anchor sunk by a local underwater historical society. Local fishermen and members of the Madawaska diving community have good reason to identify the wreckage.

The encrusted, embattered *Mayflower* sits in a wide expanse of sand. The plant growth on her timber has made her an oasis of green and brown in a sand and water desert. The fish have come to look upon the *Mayflower* as a supermarket for algae and nibble-size plant food. A diver can always count on seeing hundreds upon hundreds of fish swimming around the boiler, flitting through the rotting dual sternwheel and basking along the *Mayflower's* long-empty deck.

For anglers, the *Mayflower* is a prime location for hunting bass. There is a huge school of big bass, some as large as five pounds, continuously milling about the broken bits of the ship. Lake trout, yellow pickerel, pike, whitefish and the ever-present pumpkinseed flit about the rusting, rotting hulk.

Since the wreck is located in the main traffic channel of the lake, the marker is not always to be found. The buoy, usually a Javex bottle tied by a rope to the anchor, is often knocked off its moorings by night-time speedboaters who whiz by, oblivious to what lies beneath the waves.

To be technical, the expert way to locate the *Mayflower* is through an oft-used siting. Draw a straight line in an easterly direction from the northern top of Parcher Island, past the southern end of Mayflower Island on towards three large rocks on the edge of the eastern shore line. At a point two thirds of the distance from Mayflower Island to

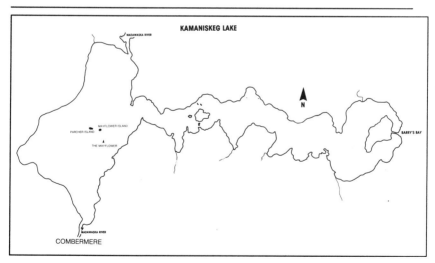

**On the night of November 12, 1912, the *Mayflower* travelled from Barry's Bay (far right of the map) west towards the open section of Lake Kamaniskeg. The ship foundered near what is now Mayflower Island. The village of Combermere is at the bottom of the map. The wreck site is only an approximation — scuba divers should not use it for locating the *Mayflower*.**

the three rocks lies the *Mayflower*. She sits in twenty to twenty-five feet of water on a sand bottom.

Sound scientific? Well, in all honesty, without the markers it is difficult to pinpoint the *Mayflower* on first try. This author once had to snorkel for ten minutes in the waters around the wreck before the bones of the ship were found. Divers need only be patient; their search will be rewarded.

Getting to the wreck is a scenic voyage that will enthrall divers. Barry's Bay rests on a long thin bay (aptly called Barry's Bay), six miles from the main body of Kamaniskeg Lake. The town is tucked away on the northern tip of the bay. There is a large tooth-shaped island blocking the village's view of the open fresh-water fjord. Mask Island is large enough to support a number of farms; along the shore are cottages and a marina.

**The waters of Lake Kamaniskeg are tea coloured. For underwater photography, the best visibility is in the spring. Above, author Stephen Weir loads this Barry's Bay dive boat for a trip to the *Mayflower*. The photograph was taken early in May, one week after the ice had left the lake.**

Photograph — Maria Nenadovich

On a recent outing, a dive party left for the *Mayflower* from Barry's Bay. The flat-bottom dive boat had been rented at the marina on Mask Island. The seven-mile run from the dock to Mayflower Island was a colourful journey. The skies were clear and the sun's rays brought out the rich blue tones of the lake in spring. Along the shore the reflection of the green-budded trees and white/black rock was perfect, there wasn't another craft on the water to ripple this natural mirror.

Little has changed on the lake in the past seventy-six years. There are but a few cottages dotting the twenty-nine miles of shore line that encircle this seventy-two-hundred-acre lake. Summer retreats have replaced the logging camps and pioneer farms of the nineteenth century.

Few roads lead down to the water's edge. The high hills and thick pine forest have discouraged a massive cottage invasion. Hence the trip south along the lake is a skiff ride past a wall of rock and wood, a scene not unlike what the passengers aboard the *Mayflower* took in during her regular daylight runs.

The voyage lasts forty minutes. When a course is set to run up the middle of the Barry's Bay tongue, the craft passes easily between the steep hills that line Bleskie's Point on the west shore and Blueberry Point to the east. Below, the water is eighty feet in depth, no need to worry about running aground out here.

Piloting the dive boat only becomes a tricky task when one approaches the Narrows, the section of the lake where Barry's Bay breaks off from the deep main body of Lake Kamaniskeg.

The Narrows, as the name implies, is a thin passageway and is also very shallow. At its narrowest, the main traffic lane shrinks to one-tenth-of-a-mile wide and the depth is a prop-pranging ten feet. The danger zone is rounding Ski Island, a small drop of land that all but fills the top end of the Narrows. It has shoals that can easily take the bottom out of a fast-moving pleasure boat when the water levels are down.

The wreck of the *Mayflower* usually has a marker attached to it to help divers and fishermen locate the wreck. Oftentimes the locals use the *Mayflower's* boiler to attach a marker. In recent years, Save Ontario Shipwrecks has installed a marker beside the wreck in an attempt to save the remains of the *Mayflower* from anchor damage.

Photograph - S. Weir

Before the days when the levels of the lake were controlled, dredging had to be done in this area to free up the channel.

Once past the Narrows, the lake opens to its fullest. Filled constantly by the incoming waters of the Madawaska River to the north-east, the lake bottom drops to, at places,one hundred and thirty feet.

In spring the waters of Lake Kamaniskeg are clear, making the wreck easier to spot. But the water levels tend to be much higher in May and June, and that can hamper the search for the ship. By the first of June there is a marker on the wreck.

The second way to visit the *Mayflower* is to launch a boat from Sand Bay. There is a private park across the lake and south of the wreck site. It is not as pretty a boat ride to the hulk, but by leaving from Sand Bay one saves gas and time.

The bones of the stern-wheeler are but a scant two-mile run from Sand Bay. It is an easy trip even for the slowest moving punt. And, unlike the route from Barry's Bay, this trip is over deep water, no need to look for near-surface hazards.

A third route? Divers can launch at a public dock in Combermere and travel up the Madawaska River, a route the *Mayflower* often took.

In summer, the warm weather makes scuba diving comfortable. However, the heat also increases plant growth in the water and visibility is clouded by a brown haze. For photographers, the best time is spring or fall.

It is a quick feather fall from the boat to the bottom of the lake. The *Mayflower* sits upright on a wide expanse of sand, flat rocks and broken pieces of lumber.

Lying on the sand beside the wooden hull of the *Mayflower*, a diver's depth guage reads twenty-five feet. At the top of her rusting boiler, she's only ten feet from the surface.

At one time the flagstaff of the *Mayflower* poked right out of the water. Years of freezes and thaws have destroyed the upper deck and pilot-house of the *Mayflower*, and, the most unkind cut of all, the ship was dynamited after the First World War. The sand around the hulk is covered in wood, the remains of the upper reaches of the ship.

The boiler, vestiges of the sternwheel and the solid wooden hull are still to be seen. There should be more, but the *Mayflower* has been picked over by wave after wave of souvenir-seeking aquanauts. The only way to see all of the ship would be to tour the garages and the rec-room bars of the people who have dived on the ship over the last twenty years. Gone are the ship's wheel, the furniture, the windows and even much of the ship's deck material.

"When I first went out to the *Mayflower* twenty-seven years ago, she was almost intact," recalled Barry's Bay dive-boat owner Bob Atchson. But that was long before sport diving had really caught on in the Ottawa Valley.

**An encrusted boiler pipe sits on the bottom of Lake Kamaniskeg amid pieces of broken wood from the wheel-house of the steamship *Mayflower*.**

Photograph - S. Weir

In the 1970s, a scuba diver found an unopened bottle of whisky in the wreck. That find helped to accelerate the stripping of the *Mayflower*. The rumoured cache of a whisky cargo was, of course, never found. However, treasure seekers managed to take everything that could be manhandled to the surface.

The Madawaska Valley Tourist Council and the SOS (Save Ontario Shipwrecks) are working to save what is left of the Kamaniskeg lady. Every visitor to the *Mayflower* now sees a large metal sign nailed to the floor boards of her still strong hull.

**The Save Ontario Shipwrecks Association has made a study of the *Mayflower* wreck. The grid wires still criss-cross the deck of the sunken steamer. The grid wires were used to section off the ship so that sector-by-sector photographs of the *Mayflower* could be taken.**

Photograph - S. Weir

The message reads: "Welcome to the *Mayflower*. Divers please respect this historic site. Do not dismantle parts from the boat. Madawaska Valley Tourist Council."

The metal message isn't the only sign of man's effort to preserve the remains of the *Mayflower*. An underwater archeological survey of the ship has been made. The grid wires from that study are still in place, running the breadth and width of the deck. A number of television items, radio stories, newspaper articles and magazine features have appeared concerning the *Mayflower*. There is enthusiasm in the Barry's Bay/Combermere area to preserve what is left of the ghost ship.

What makes the *Mayflower* so susceptible to damage is her shallow depth. Down twenty-five feet, the ruined stern-wheeler is an easy dive, even for the most novice of scuba divers. A steady stream of visitors will take its toll on any historical attraction.

Also, at that depth the *Mayflower* is in relatively warm water, above the lake's thermocline. A Ministry of Natural Resources survey in 1975 found that the temperature near the surface was an average sixty-six degrees Fahrenheit, while near the bottom, at one hundred and thirty feet, the thermometer dropped to a chilly forty degrees Fahrenheit.

At twenty-five feet, with warm temperatures and a steady diet of sunlight, there has been a riotous growth of plant life on the timbers of the ship. Rotting has taken place and the deck is covered in a blanket of fur. The boiler is covered in a layer of growing algae. In recent years a new menace has also caused damage: the effects of acid rain are showing on the metal bits of the *Mayflower*.

The best time to visit the wreck is in the fall. The woods around Combermere are ablaze with colour in late September.

The still waters of the lake throw back an image filled with bright reds, warm yellows and dusty browns.

It is a time of year when the tourists have gone home. There are few boats out to disturb the waters above the *Mayflower*. If a dive party is lucky, the temperatures of the air and the water rival the hottest days of summer.

The conditions can be perfect for an underwater photo session. The sediment caused by the activities of summer has settled to the bottom. The algae that blooms in July has, for the most part, slowed down. The water temperature, at seventy-two degrees, is still very warm — divers will not need to wear hoods or gloves. The visability in the fall is always acceptable.

Photographers will need to take a flash or use a very high speed film. The nearby Parcher and Mayflower Islands are excellent beach points for scuba parties to suit up and load film.

Of course, the best time to capture the *Mayflower* on film is in the winter, when the sediment is gone from the water. The lake freezes over in December, so a winter visit is left to chainsaw-carrying scuba clubs.

# THE LAST CHAPTER

The rotting hulk of the *Mayflower* is more than just a side-show attraction for weekend scuba divers. The wood and steel remains are, to some, a historical time capsule.

Picking through the decaying bones of the wooden ship, one is able to catch glimpses of how life was back in 1912. The design and the subsequent modifications to the *Mayflower* were extremely backwoods. A study of the ship's design shows that, for the likes of Jack Hudson, the whole business of running a steamship line was very much done by the seat of the pants. His spirit and

**The centre of the paddle-wheel is now completely encrusted in rust and aquatic plant life.**

Photograph — S. Weir

his willingness to challenge the elements in the makeshift *Mayflower* mirror the pioneer spirit of the Upper Ottawa Valley.

Sport divers can only get a vague feel for the nature of the vessel when swimming along her now empty decks. It is up to the underwater marine archaeologist to really understand the historical importance of the wreck.

Save Ontario Shipwrecks (SOS), a province-wide group dedicated to preserving Ontario's marine heritage, spent 1985 to 1987 examining, photographing and cataloging every inch of the *Mayflower* wreck.

SOS's Ottawa Valley chapter sent its scuba-diving historians onto the wooden remains of the ship with grid

**A diver takes a close-up look at the paddle-wheel on the wreck of the *Mayflower*. The tea-coloured waters of Lake Kamaniskeg make for dark dives, even at a depth of only twenty feet.**

Photograph — S. Weir

wires and cameras. The divers placed lines across the hull in regular intervals so that a composite photograph and drawings of the ship could accurately be done.

The SOS experts worked under licence from the Ministry of Citizenship and Culture in their study of the ship. Their files are now so complete they probably know more about the ship than the Hudson brothers did when she was built.

The marine-archaeology group has kept its findings on file and will in all likelihood publish a paper on the *Mayflower*.

In the fall 1987 SOS newsletter, published quarterly by the provincial group, the Ottawa Valley chapter presented a short article on the history of the sinking of the *Mayflower*.

Their findings? For the most part the group agreed that the ship had sunk due to an opening of the seams in the hull.

**The rusted strut of the badly damaged *Mayflower* paddle-wheel.**

Photograph — S. Weir

"So while the theory of water rushing in very rapidly through the open seams appears borne out by the evidence, the question of how two feet of freeboard could have been lost before it was noticed that water was pouring in remains a puzzle. It is an especially vexing question as five men, including the captain and fireman, were grouped around the boiler housing at the time and the furnace door through which Delaney must have been pretty constantly shoving soft slabwood was only eighteen inches from the bottom of the boat."

The group has already placed a mooring ring and float near the *Mayflower*, allowing dive groups to tie their boats without having to drop damaging anchors onto the fragile deck of the wreck. This action alone has extended the life of the *Mayflower* — a falling ten pounds of lead can cause major harm to a rotting shipwreck. Plans call for the underwater historians to place a commemorative plaque on the deck of the *Mayflower* to let sport divers know the history of this fascinating wreck.

By 1989 the investigation of the remains had all but ended. Historical conservationists are now trying to catalogue and investigate all shipwrecks in the Ottawa Valley. Scuba divers interested in the *Mayflower* should also dive near the Hudson Hotel in Combermere. The Hudson brothers had a number of vessels before the *Mayflower*. The ships were used until they no longer were seaworthy. These decommissioned boats were then dragged onto the hotel property shore line and left to rot.

In 1911, the hotel and the retired Hudson fleet fell victim to flames. The remains of the ships and some of the original hotel can be seen underwater. The sandy bottom of the Madawaska River is littered with debris from that era. Broken hand-blown bottles, charred pieces of deck and shards of pottery are readily found by divers visiting the site. The dive locale is just up river from the Highway 62 bridge that spans the Madawaska River. The water is accessible from the parking lot of Jack Hudson's old hostelry.

The Hudson hotel is now easy to identify. The building, left in ruins in the 70s, was restored in 1986 to a condition that probably exceeds her condition when originally built in 1911.

The two-storey inn is now a restaurant and bar called the Hudson House. A picture of John Hudson hangs in the main hall.

There are other reminders of the *Mayflower* tragedy still to be seen. The O'Brien Hotel is now part of the Madonna House Museum and Catholic Retreat. The Balmoral Hotel is still in active service and is worth visiting, if for nothing else than to see the painting by local artist Frank Ritza depicting the four survivors clinging to Brown's coffin.

Even the Balmoral Hotel's registry, which was used in 1912 by the

**This sign outside the Hudson House has a stylized picture of the *Mayflower* — she never looked that good in real life!**

Photograph — B. Weir

investigators to determine who had been on board the
*Mayflower* when she went down, has survived. According
to a story in the Barry's Bay newspaper, the registry, kept
by then-owner Mark Billing, recorded the business that
transpired between Billing and Hudson. The newspaper
lists, from the registry, entries for November 1906. In that
month the *Mayflower* missed five days of travel between
Combermere and Barry's Bay (excluding Sundays); as far
as the rest of the month was concerned Hudson delivered
sixty-one loads of freight including three loads of 'drawing
beer.' Hudson and his crew ate twenty-six meals at the hotel
in November 1906 at twenty-five cents a meal.

Hudson often stayed in Barry's Bay at the Balmoral Hotel.
But, when it came time to bury him, he was interred in

**Jack Hudson's mother owned and operated a Madawaska
riverside hotel. The two-storey brick hotel was in ruins for twenty
years. It has recently been restored and houses a restaurant aptly
named the Hudson House.**

Photograph — S. Weir

Combermere, his offical home. His grave is in a cemetery within sight of the hotel. The bodies of the other victims, save for Bothwell, are in graveyards near Combermere and Barry's Bay.

And what of the survivors? Little is known about what happened to two of the three salesmen. With each passing year, Peverly and Imlach faded from the public eye. Not so with Harper. The survivor who burned his feet in the fire returned to Lake Kamaniskeg several times after the tragedy. The Barry's Bay newspaper interviewed Harper years after the mishap. Harper's son, John, also visited Barry's Bay and the local newspaper photographed him holding the lighter Harper used to start a fire on Gull Island.

**Mrs. Jean Richter (right) sits with Margaret Hudson, the widow of John Hudson. The photograph was taken on the fiftieth anniversary of the sinking of the *Mayflower*.**

Photograph — Jean Richter Collection

Margaret Hudson stayed in Combermere following the death of her husband. She ran the hotel throughout the forties and fifties and died in 1970. She was very close to the church and was well loved by the people of the Madonna House. Her grave is close to the retreat along the banks of the Madawaska River, a few miles from where her late husband was buried. On her tombstone is mention of her husband, "Captain John Hudson."

**Jack Hudson was an Anglican, his wife a Catholic. He was buried in the Anglican cemetery and his wife was laid to rest several miles away in a cemetery close to the Catholic Madonna House retreat.**

Photograph — S. Weir

Maggie and John's only son, Edwin Hudson, was raised in Combermere. He, according to a biography printed in the Barry's Bay paper, *This Week*, studied to be a dentist, dropping out just months before graduation.

In 1942, Edwin became the reeve of Radcliffe Township, like his father before him. He eventually moved to Toronto where he worked as a tax specialist. Upon his retirement he returned to Combermere to look after his mother.

Mrs Hudson had seen the reputation

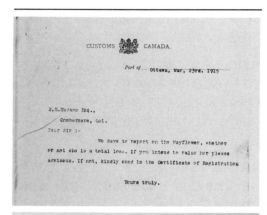

of her husband tarnished during the inquiry. Over the next fifty years she saw the Hudson name come back into respect. People began to stress the heroic nature of the man. In the sixties, two poems were written about the

**Early in 1915 the customs office wrote to Mrs. John Hudson asking her if she planned to raise the *Mayflower*. She replied, in February of that year, that she had sold the rights to the *Mayflower* to her brother-in-law, Hal Hudson. The customs department, receiving Mrs. Hudson's reply, dutifully wrote Hal Hudson asking what he planned to do. Hudson scrawled back a note saying he planned to raise her that year. His salvage attempts obviously failed.**

Canadian Archives RG 42
Volume 1784

*Mayflower* and now a five-part CBC radio drama is in the works.

Henry Hudson continued to live in the Barry's Bay area and apparently continued to operate steamships on Lake Kamaniskeg. He is listed as the last owner of the *Ruby* when the Barry's Bay steamship was decommissioned in 1920.

The National Archives uncovered in 1987 a long forgotten cache of government files. Included in the find was a report on the salvage rights of the *Mayflower* following her sinking.

In the eyes of the law the *Mayflower* belonged to John Hudson's widow. She was contacted in 1915 by the government as to her intentions regarding the wreck.

She wrote back to the Collector of Customs in February of that year thusly: "I sold my interest in the *Mayflower* to Mr. H. E. 'Henry' Hudson of this town and cannot say whether he intends raising her or not. Would refer you to him for any information you wish to know concerning the *Mayflower.*"

On March 23, 1915, a clerk from Customs Canada did just that. F. M. Jurneaux wrote to Henry Hudson in Combermere asking what was to happen to the *Mayflower*. "If you intend to raise her please advise us," wrote the clerk, "if not kindly send in the certificate of registration."

Henry wrote a very short note back stating: "I intend to make another attempt to salvage her and if unsuccessful will send in certificate."

The file includes the ship's certificate, but there is no date attached to tell us when Hudson gave up his salvage attempts. Presumably it was late in 1915.

The wreck was undisturbed for thirty years. The bow pole continued to stick out of the water for years. After the war, the wreck was dynamited to clear the boat channel.

In 1967 the township of Radcliffe opened the Mayflower Centennial Park marking and honouring those who were lost in the November 12, 1912 mishap. The grandchildren of Mrs. William McWhirter had a cairn built and placed in the park.

The bronze plaque on the stone monument marks the date of the disaster and lists the names of those who died on the *Mayflower*.

Two years after the park was opened, the Geographical Board of Canada, at the urging of Mrs. Jean Richter (a relative of Aaron Parcher) and the township of Radcliffe, renamed Gull Island, where the survivors landed, Mayflower Island. A second smaller island beside it was named Parcher Island.

A look at a Renfrew County map shows that the names of the principals in this long-ago drama live on. There is Paddy's Road (after Paddy O'Brien), Parcher Point, Boehme's Mountain, Boehme's Pond and Hudson Pond.

When the conservation group has placed its plaque upon the deck of the *Mayflower*, the story will finally be complete.

The *Mayflower* will then be remembered in art, in mind and in the written word... a testament to the unsinkable spirit of the pioneer days of Renfrew County.

# Ripley's — Believe It or Not!®

**THE CORPSE THAT SAVED 3 MEN FROM DROWNING!**
THE STEAMER "MAYFLOWER"
SANK IN LAKE KAMANISKEG, ONTARIO, DROWNING 9 PERSONS,
INCLUDING ITS OWNER AND ITS CAPTAIN, BUT 3 PASSENGERS
SURVIVED BY LASHING THEIR HANDS TOGETHER
*ACROSS THE TOP OF A COFFIN IN WHICH A BODY
WAS BEING TRANSPORTED FOR BURIAL* (Nov. 12,1912)

**The story of the *Mayflower* continues to interest people decades
after the ship went down. In 1971, *Ripley's Believe It or Not*
featured the wreck in one of their columns.**

# APPENDIX ONE

## Important Information For Divers:

Lake Kamaniskeg is approximately 140 km north-west of the city of Ottawa and 225 km north-east of Toronto. To reach the lake from Ottawa travellers should drive north from the capital on Highway 417/17 and take Highway 60 west just outside of Renfrew.

From Toronto divers should travel east on Highway 401 and take Highway 28 north. In Bancroft the *Mayflower*-bound travellers should take Highway 62. Highways 62 and 60 meet in Barry's Bay on the shores of Lake Kamaniskeg.

## Services:

Combermere and Barry's Bay sport modern tourist facilities. There are campsites, hotels, motels and resorts on Lake Kamaniskeg and the Madawaska River. Dive boats can be rented from the following establishments:

- **Sand Bay Camp**, Kamaniskeg Road South, RR 2, Combermere, Ontario, 613-756-3505.
- **Opeongo Trail Resort**, Highway 62, Combermere, Ontario, 613-756-3509.
- **Riverview Motel**, Highway 62, Combermere, Ontario, 613-756-3633.
- **Stevenson Lodge**, Highway 517, RR 2, Combermere, Ontario, 613-756-3505.

## Diving Services:

There are presently no facilities near Lake Kamaniskeg to fill tanks or to rent dive gear. Divers should bring all their own gear. The closest Ontario Underwater Council approved air fill stations are:

- **Black Bay Recreation Inc.**, RR 1, Petawawa, Ontario, 613-687-4448.
- **Ontario Divers**, 1040 Lansdowne St West, Peterborough, Ontario, 705-743-1015.

# APPENDIX TWO

There are now no commercial ships working the waters of Lake Kamaniskeg, Bark Lake or the Upper Madawaska River. In the twenty years surrounding both sides of the turn of the century there were an estimated dozen ships carrying passengers, herding lumber and hauling freight.

In this history of the *Mayflower*, reference is made to five vessels that saw active service in and around Barry's Bay and Combermere. What follows is information gathered in part by the National Archives and by local marine historians regarding the five ships.

● **Hudson**. The Hudson brothers began their shipping interests in 1899 when they built the paddle-wheel steamer the *Hudson*. She was 73.5 feet by 17 feet by 3.3 feet. She was 36.51 tonnage registered (44.81 gross tons). She had a 24 inch stroke, 60-horsepower engine that John Hudson purchased from the Canadian Locomotive and Engine Works in Kingston in 1899. According to local historian Howard Magda, the *Hudson* had paddle-wheels on both sides of her. She was apparently decommissioned in 1904. The Hudson brothers, Hal and Jack, the registered owners, (each had thirty-two shares in the ownership of the *Hudson*) pulled her onto land near their Combermere Hotel, and she was lost in the fire of 1911.

- **The Mayflower.** The *Mayflower* was built in
Combermere by Napoleon Tessier in 1903. The Hull,
Quebec boat builder constructed the 77-foot-long
stern-wheel paddler, the two vertical engines were
installed by the Montreal firm J&R Weir. The *Mayflower*
had two decks, a draft of 4 feet and was 18 feet wide. Her
gross tonnage was 58.86 tons and her registered tonnage
was 38.02 tons. The *Mayflower* was launched in 1904
shortly before the *Ruby* was put into service.

- **E. L. Perkins.** Built in 1887 by Alfred Driscoll (Aylmer,
Quebec) this vessel measured 45 feet by 8 feet, 6 inches,
by 6 feet, 2 inches. She weighed in at 17.45 gross tons
and 15.91 tons registered. The first owner of the *Perkins*
was Edward Lyman Perkins, hence the name of the ship.
Driscoll died in 1892 and the ownership of the boat was
transferred to his wife, Eleanor Conroy. In 1894, David
Johnson of Combermere acquired title to the vessel. She
apparently sank in the Madawaska River, a few miles
south of the *Mayflower*. Her registry was closed off on 7
June 1895.

- **Pioneer.** The *Pioneer* was built on Bark Lake by J&R
Weir of Montreal; the same firm that worked on the
*Mayflower's* engines. The *Pioneer* was built in 1888 and
according to government records she weighed 37.25 tons
gross, 25.6 tons registered and her dimensions were 59
feet, 5 inches by 14 feet, 5 inches by 6 feet, 2 inches. The
ship had one deck, a mast and a rounded stern. The
vessel was owned by Godfrey Benning, a principal of the
Madawaska Improvement Company. The *Pioneer* sank in
Bark Lake and she was deregistered November 1904.

- **Ruby.** The *Ruby* was built in Barry's Bay by Napoleon
Tessier, the same man who built the *Mayflower*. The Hull,
Quebec boat builder completed the *Ruby* in 1903. A
steam-screw, she weighed 11.12 tons gross and 8.79

tons registered. She measured 41 feet, 6 inches by 9 feet, 3 inches by 4 feet. The *Ruby* had a fan stern and one deck. The ship was registered in 1904 to the Canada Corundum Company. In September 1914 the company sold the *Ruby* to Henry Hudson. She was dismantled and her registry closed in January 1919.

• **Tiger.** The author has not been able to find much information about the *Tiger* (or *Tyger*). The ship was built in 1896 in Lakeport, USA. She was 34 feet long, 7.5 feet wide. The ship had a draft of 3 feet and could carry 3 tons of cargo. Newspaper reports of the day describe her as being smaller than the *Ruby*. The *Tiger* was, reportedly, a gas-driven ship but it has also been called a steam driven ship, and was used in conjunction with the *Ruby* in the services of the Ontario Corundum Company Limited of Ottawa, Ontario. By 1920 the *Tiger* was delisted from the federal government's list of steam vessels.

# BIBLIOGRAPHY

## BOOKS

1.  AUDET, Francois J. Canadian Historical Dates & Events 1492-1915. Ottawa, Ontario. 1917. Beuregard Publishing.
2.  BANCROFT Senior Citizens. Carlaw Township, Before the Memories Fade. Bancroft, Ontario. 1977 2nd printing 1984. Bancroft Times Publishing.
3.  BARRY, James. Wrecks and Rescues on the Great Lakes. La Jolla California. 1980. Howell North Books.
4.  BOWEN, Dana Thomas. Shipwrecks of the Lakes.
5.  BROWN, Ron. Backroads of Ontario. Edmonton, Alberta. 1984 Hurtig Publishers Limited
6.  BRIDGEWATER, William. Editor. Columbia Viking Desk Encyclopedia. New York, NY.1953. Viking Press.
7.  CHAMBERS, Earnest. Editor. Canadian Parliamentary Guide-1913. 1913. Ottawa Ont. 1913. Mortimer Co. Ltd.
8.  CHAMBERS, Earnest. Editor. Canadian Parliamentary Guide - 1917. Ottawa, Ont. 1917. Mortimer Co. Ltd.
9.  CHURCH, Les & Aledene. Births, Marriages and Deaths; Abstracts from the Renfrew Mercury. Burnstown, Ontario 1984. General Store Publishing.
10. COULL, John. Wrecks of the St. Lawrence River and Lake Ontario. Toronto, Ontario. Edited by Stephen J. Weir. pending (1988). publishers: Ontario Underwater Council.

11. Debates, House of Commons. Session 1912-13
    Volume 11. Ottawa, Ontario. 1913. Queen's Printer.
12. Department of Marine & Fisheries. Steam and Sail
    Registry. Ottawa, Ontario. 1895. Queen's Printer.
13. Dominion of Canada Guide Book - containing
    information for intending settlers. Ottawa, Ontario. 1883.
    Queen's Printer.
14. Early Days in Ottawa County, a Short History of
    Ottawa, Hull and the National Capital Region. Ottawa,
    Ontario. 1971 (reprint of 1967 original edition).
    Published by the National Capital Commission.
15. FINNIGAN, Joan. Giants of Canada's Ottawa Valley.
    Burnstown, Ontario. 1980. General Store Publishing.
16. FINNIGAN, Joan. Some of the Stories I Told You Were
    True. Ottawa, Ontario. 1981. Deneau Publishing and
    Company Limited.
17. FREEMAN, B.C. Mineral Deposits in Renfrew County
    and Vicinity. Ottawa, Ontario. 1936. Canada
    Department of Mines. Memoir 195. King's Printer.
18. HAMILTON, William. MacMillan Book of Canadian
    Place Names. Toronto, Ontario. 1978. MacMillan of
    Canada. ISBN 0-7706
19. HERTIG,MEL.Canadian Encyclopedia. Edmonton,
    Alberta. 1985. Hertig Publishing Limited.
20. IVONOFFSKI, Vrenia and Sandra Campbell. Exploring
    Our Heritage: The Ottawa Valley Experience. Arnprior,
    Ontario. 1980. Published by the Arnprior and District
    Historical Society.
21. KENNEDY, Clyde C.. Upper Ottawa Valley, a Glimpse
    of History. Pembroke, Ontario. 1970. Published by the
    Renfrew County Council.
22. KENNEDY, Clyde C. & Mrs Carl Price. Notes on the
    History of Renfrew County for the Centennial 1961.
    Pembroke, Ontario. 1961. Published by the Renfrew
    County Council.

23. LAROUSSE. Larousse Illustrated International
    Encyclopedia and Dictionary. New York, NY. 1972.
    McGraw Hill Publishing Ltd.
24. LEE-WHITING, Brenda. Harvest of Stones; the
    German Settlement in Renfrew County. Toronto, Ont.
    1985. University of Toronto Press.
25. LEGGET, Robert. Ottawa Waterways, Gateway to a
    Continent. Toronto, Ont. 1975. University of Toronto Press.
26. MACPHERSON, K.R. World Ship Society Preliminary
    List of Canadian Merchant Steamships 1809-1930.
    Toronto, Ontario. 1962. Published by the Toronto Branch
    of the World Ship Society.
27. MADAWASKA TOURIST ASSOCIATION. Guide Book
    #16. Pembroke, Ontario. 1952. Pembroke Standard
    Publishing.
28. MORGAN, H.R. Steam Navigation on the Ottawa River
    - Ontario, Historical Society Papers and Records
    Volume XXIII. Toronto, Ontario. 1926. Published
    by the OHS.
29. MYERS, JAY. Canadian Facts and Dates. 1986.
    Fitzhenry & Whiteside Ltd. Markham, Ontario
30. Ministry of Culture and Recreation. Ontario Historic
    Sites, Museums, Galleries and Plaques. Toronto, Ontario.
    1978. Published by the Ontario Provincial Government .
31. Official Report of the Debates of the House of Commons.
    67 Session. 12th Parliament 6-7 George V. 1916. Volume
    CXXII. Ottawa,Ontario. 1917. King's Printer.
32. STEINBERG, S. Historical Tables. 58 BC-AD 1972.
    Ironbridge. UK. 1973. MacMillan Press.
33. TAPLIN, Glen. Canadian Chronology. Metuchen, New
    Jersey. 1970. Scarecrow Press.
34. WALKER, Harry. Renfrew and It's Fair Through 100
    Years. Renfrew, Ontario. 1953. Published by the
    Renfrew Agricultural Society.
35. WEIR, Stephen J. & Bruce Paton. The History of
    Renfrew County. Renfrew, Ontario. 1973. Unpublished.

## NEWSPAPERS AND MAGAZINES

**Belleville Intelligencer**. Weekly. Belleville, Ontario.
**Dayton Daily.** Dayton, Ohio.
**Eganville Leader**. Weekly. Eganville, Ontario.
**Montreal Star**. Daily, Montreal, Quebec.
**Ontario Reformer**. Oshawa, Ontario.
**Orono News**. Weekly. Orono, Ontario.
**Oshawa Daily Times**. Daily. Oshawa, Ontario.
**Ottawa Evening Journal**. Daily. Ottawa, Ontario
**Ottawa Journal**. Daily. Ottawa, Ontario.
**Pembroke Observer**. Daily. Pembroke, Ontario.
**Pembroke Standard**. Weekly. Pembroke, Ontario.
**Peterborough Examiner**. Daily. Peterborough, Ontario
**Port Hope Guide**. Weekly. Port Hope, Ontario.
**Regina Saskatchewan Leader**. Daily. Regina, Sask.
**This Week In The Madawaska Valley**. Weekly. Barry's
Bay, Ontario.

## MANUSCRIPT, PAMPHLETS AND BROCHURES

CITY OF PEMBROKE. Canada's Next City -
Pembroke.1915. Pamphlet published by Desmond D.
Morris. Pembroke, Ontario.
INLAND WATERWAYS OF CANADA. 1913. Berlin,
Ontario. Pamphlet published by the Great Waterways
Union of Canada.
LIST OF STEAM VESSELS. 1919. Sessional Paper No 22.
King's Printer. Ottawa, Ontario.
MADAWASKA IMPROVEMENT COMPANY LIMITED.
Papers, letters and corporate records. January 21 1886 -
1905. Ottawa, Ontario.
MADONNA HOUSE MUSEUM. Various clippings file.
Combermere, Ontario.

METRO TORONTO REFERENCE LIBRARY. Selected
Shipwrecks Record.1901-1936. Microfiche. Toronto,
Ontario. F N5583 V 333-335
ONTARIO ARCHIVES. Marine Protest Affidavit. MS 635
ONTARIO ARCHIVES. Steamship Scrapbook. Various
clippings. MS 419
ONTARIO ARCHIVES. Renfrew Historical Clippings. MV
2636
ONTARIO ARCHIVES. Dunn Papers. MU 1999
ONTARIO ARCHIVES. Map of Crown Land. 1860.
Radcliffe Township. C-37.
ONTARIO ARCHIVES. Radcliffe Township Land Grants.
microfilm.
ONTARIO ARCHIVES. Radcliffe Township Voters List
1902. 1919. Mun. Doc.
ONTARIO ARCHIVES. Pamphlets - 1883. #3
PUBLIC ARCHIVES OF CANADA. Department of Marine
and Fisheries. Various documents relating to the
investigation of the loss of the Mayflower. R.G. 42.
Volume 206. File #33435
PUBLIC ARCHIVES OF CANADA. Wreck Report and
Misc. Documents. RG 42. Volume 1784.
RENFREW. 1958 Renfrew Centennial Official Program.
Renfrew, Ontario. 1958. Published by town of Renfrew.
SAVE ONTARIO SHIPWRECKS. Newsletter. Fall 1987. St.
Catharines Ontario. Article: The 'Mayflower' Tragedy - a
75th Anniversary Perspective by James Anderson.
VOTER'S LIST RADCLIFFE TOWNSHIP. The Year 1902.
1902. Ottawa. Ontario. Queen's Printer.
VOTER'S LIST RADCLIFFE TOWNSHIP. The Year 1919.
1919. Ottawa, Ontario. King's Printer.
WATERWAYS OF CANADA. A sail to the Rockies. 1897. A
special pamphlet in a number of Ontario newspapers.

## UNPUBLISHED LETTERS & MISC. ITEMS

Unpublished Letters Of Howard Magda
Unpublished Letters Of Jean Ritcher
Unpublished Letter Of Arthur Rumleski
Unpublished Letters Of The SOS
CBC Tape-Ottawa Radio Mini-doc 1985

# ABOUT THE AUTHOR

Stephen Weir was raised in the Ottawa Valley. Since graduating in 1975 from Toronto's Ryerson Polytechnical Institute (Journalism), he has worked and written for radio stations, television stations, newspapers, magazines and corporate publications in Windsor, Lakefield and Toronto.

Stephen and his wife, Marie Nenadovich, learned to dive in 1978. They have dived extensively throughout the Caribbean, the Great Lakes and the North Pacific. No matter how far afield their hobby takes them, they always return each summer to the Ottawa Valley to explore the lakes and rivers around Combermere and Eganville.

Photograph—Cindy Gordon

Stephen's magazine articles have appeared in publications throughout North America. He wrote a half-hour radio documentary about the sinking of the Great Lakes steamship, the *Price*. It was produced and aired by a Toronto radio station in 1985. He has edited and assisted in a number of non-fiction works — this is his first book.

Stephen works as a public-relations officer for a large aerospace firm in Etobicoke, Ontario. He lives in Toronto's Cabbagetown with his wife and their two children, Michael and Andrew.